Practicing Happy

Timothy Daulter

DEDICATION

To Anni, Zoë, Lotus, Bodhi & River

CONTENTS

Acknowledgments i

1 Happy Is As Happy Does 1

2 Wake Up! 9

3 The Simple Choice 21

4 Change the Software 30

5 The Path 38

6 The Happiness Workout 60

7 Wrapping It All Up 85

ACKNOWLEDGMENTS

Practicing Happy has only been possible due to the many gifts of wisdom, knowledge and support that I have received over the last five years. I am especially grateful to my wife, Anni, who helped me to go deeper into this path, relayed information and inspiration from Spirit (even when I was not listening or did not want to hear it) and was a constant source of support, especially when I was doubting myself. Thank you also to all of my teachers, including: Jesus, Buddha, Eckhart Tolle, Gary Renard, Thom Hartmann, Alberto Villodo, Rick Jarow, Thich Nhat Hanh, Lao Tzu and, of course, The School of Hard Knocks.

CHAPTER 1

HAPPY IS AS HAPPY DOES

Introduction

It is November 2007, José and I are moving the last remaining boxes and furniture out of our commercial kitchen. This all started three and a half years earlier after I was fired from my job for trying to do the right thing. A few months into my unemployment my first child was born and my wife, Anni, and I started our dream company to make and sell top quality fresh baby food. We cashed out our 401(k)s, borrowed from everyone who was willing and a few who were reluctant and launched in the direction of our dreams. Over the next few years we had our struggles, cars repossessed at the worst possible times, living with the stress of no health insurance for our small children and a constant battle to keep a roof over our heads and food on the table. However, in 2006 things finally seemed to have turned, the company was growing, we started selling through Whole Foods Markets® and we had a deal for the financing that we thought would put us over the hump.

Then, the financing disappeared and the deal we made prevented us from getting any additional money for the company. Instead of listening to my better business sense and cutting the losses, we propped up the company with everything that we had desperately hoping to be able to make something happen to save our dream.

On that overcast November day all hope seemed to be gone. I didn't have any money to pay José so I gave him a microwave, table and a ride home to save him bus fare. Then I went home to ponder what to do next. I had no money and no prospects and was completely physically and

1

emotionally exhausted from 3 years in the meat grinder with nothing to show for it.

I was anything but happy at this point in my life, and completely full of fear. I was afraid of not being able to make enough money to survive. I was afraid of letting down my family. I was afraid of being thought a failure. I was afraid that my life was ruined. Since all of this fear did not feel good, I also felt angry at every external factor that seemed to contribute to my situation. I was angry at our investors, I was angry at our suppliers who were suing us, I was angry at the world for not supporting this great effort and most of all I was angry at myself.

Now, jumping forward three years to November 2010, I am sitting within a circle of rocks performing a ritual designed to release the remainder of my fear. The three years since the final collapse of our company seem a lifetime ago. As I represent the release of my fears by writing them on stones, visualize the fear energy being transferred from my body to the stones and then throwing them as far as I can, I feel cleansed. I reflect on my life, the journey that I have taken and the growth that I have experienced that allowed me to progress from a depressed lost soul to someone with a purpose who is taking steps towards fulfilling my destiny.

During those interim three years much of the study that I had done over the previous 7 came together with a good deal of spiritual guidance and continued life challenges to reveal to me the truth that the difficult challenges, the tremendous successes, and everything else in my life were divine gifts. Without these specific experiences I would not have been able to grow, evolve and heal in ways that have continually raised my happiness from the depths of depression to a lightness and joy that I did not know existed. No matter what is happening, I now have the tools to be able to see the beauty in all aspects of my life. There is no better feeling than living moment to moment in love and joy, and if this sounds appealing to you (and I highly recommend it) then please read on.

Life and the Pursuit of Happiness

This book is about life. It is about how you want to experience your life and thus, ultimately, about how you choose to live. Imagine yourself in a full on love affair with your life, completely engaged in living each day and fulfilling your purpose. You are full of love and compassion for yourself and others, and you are exactly where you want to be and doing exactly what you want to do. You can have this type of life and it doesn't require magic or superhuman powers. In fact, you already have all of the tools that you need inside of you right now. So let's take a look at what happiness is, how we try to achieve it and what we actually should be doing to achieve it with a very practical step-by-step approach to get there.

The "pursuit of happiness" was listed as a basic human right when the American colonies declared independence from Britain. Just as America's founders gave voice to feelings of repression and suffering under the tyranny of a British King, each of us languishes under the despotism of our own minds. Our habitual ways of thinking and conditioned interpretations of our experiences keep us trapped in endless cycles of suffering and unhappiness. So as the Declaration of Independence proclaims the intention of the American colonies to throw off the restrictive monarchy and replace it with a government that secures their right to pursue happiness, we too must throw off our destructive ways of thinking and reacting and replace them with a thought system and practices that allow us to live in peace, joy and happiness.

The pursuit of happiness, really the pursuit of what we think will make us happy, is at the root of everything that we do in our lives. The friends that we choose, the careers and hobbies that we take up, the romantic relationships that we desire, in fact everything that we choose to do is for the sole reason of trying to make ourselves happy. Even when we choose something we don't like, for example, staying in a job that we hate, the reason is because we feel that, on balance, working at an unfulfilling and annoying job and making money will make us happier than quitting the job and dealing with the financial and social implications of being unemployed. We also are motivated to do things that we think will make our friends and family happier because it makes us happy to see our loved ones happy. Similarly, we try to crush our enemies because we think it will make us happier to see them suffer. So at the end of the day, we all may have different definitions for what "success" in our life would look like, but each person's definition of success is nothing more than what that person thinks (or has been taught) will make him or her the happiest.

So we are all living in the pursuit of happiness. While that might seem obvious, the problem is if when we are pursuing something that means that we don't yet have it. So, by definition, we aren't happy. But what does it really mean to be happy?

Definition of Happiness

In general, we call it happiness when we feel good and unhappiness when we feel bad. We feel good when our lives are filled with love, peace, security, freedom, fun and laughter and we feel bad when we are filled with fear, hate, anxiety, loneliness, depression, pain and sadness. The funny thing is that as we pursue our happy state so vigorously, these are not goals that can be achieved or things to be pursued. Happiness is our natural state of being. What we call happiness is the symptom; it is the effect, not the cause. Our job is not to seek happiness, per se, but to seek wholeness over separation and love over fear. This will return us to our natural state of being. Whenever we feel unhappy, this is a signal to us that we are not living our lives authentically, that we have lost our way and need to get back on track. So the process of living in happiness is the process of stripping away our thoughts, attitudes and actions that take us further away from our natural state of being. As we make progress in this cleansing we will return to our natural state of pure joy and bliss.

This is the journey that we are all on and is the focus of this book. I have been lucky enough to have been guided down this path in a way that has brought me from deep depression and a life that lacked meaning, purpose and joy to a place of profound reverence for my purpose here, inner peace and a deep rooted joy. I had lost all of the life from my life and now I have given myself the gift of a second chance. I often feel full of a radiant energy that makes my skin tingle and puts me in a mental place where nothing and no one can upset or bother me. I still have my share of times when I get scared, anxious, angry and even depressed, but they have become much less frequent, shorter in duration and easier to pass through. I am practicing happy every day and everyone who I come into contact with is benefiting from it.

What Does It Mean to Practice Happy?

Our lives are dominated by the pursuit of those things that we think will make us feel good: money, power, security, love, belonging, freedom, relationship, fun, entertainment, luxury, world peace, etc. and we try to avoid things that we think will make us feel bad: conflict, unpleasantness, loneliness, vulnerability, disappointment, pain, and so on. However, one problem that we all run into is that while we have some of the "good" stuff in our lives, we also have some of the "bad" stuff and our efforts to only have good stuff and no bad stuff don't work.

Even more interesting is that if we ever get a chance to hang out with people who are rich, powerful, fun, etc we will find that they don't seem to be any happier, in general, than anyone else. For example, if someone is generally unhappy before they become rich and famous then they are still unhappy after they become rich and famous, sometimes even more so.

Another problem with our basic model of happiness is that we peg our happiness to things that are outside of us and, therefore, outside of our control. In life, everyone has their victories and defeats, highs and lows, ups and downs. Many of us act as if with enough effort, we can control all of these outside forces and maintain the circumstances of our life in the perfect balance that we think will make us happy. This is a losing cause and hasn't worked for anyone yet. So the true essence of practicing happy is to figure out the fundamental factors that are in our control and that lead to happiness and in everything that we do in every moment, always choose in the direction of happiness and away from fear, anxiety and pain.

Manifesting Is Not the Answer

Happiness isn't getting what you want, it's wanting what you get.
-- *Self Help Mantra*

Recently some movements have emerged that offer the worldview that all outside events and circumstances are under our control and with the proper frame of mind and emotional state, we can visualize and manifest the outside world to fit our specifications. The inference is that by manifesting those things that we desire we will have a happier and more fulfilling life. However, I believe that the fundamental flaw with this approach is that we don't know what we truly need and what will make us happy. For example, if my 3-year-old son had his way, he would manifest candy and marshmallows for every meal, snack and dessert. But, if he were successful at this, instead of having a happier more fulfilled life, he would have significant health problems. It is the same with us. Much of the time our immediate desires are for things that we think will ease our pain or make the challenges in our lives disappear.

Spiritually speaking, much of our culture is in the stone age. We value money and fame over love and peace. We seek happiness through the physical/material world by accumulating money, things or the "perfect" set of life circumstances. These pursuits are done from an ego-centric point of view with relatively little regard for others because we see others as blocks or competitors for the material or situations that make us happy. These misunderstandings of our nature and the nature of the universe cause us to wander around, as if in the dark, with little chance of finding out way out unless we drastically alter our internal model of what is it that brings about happiness, peace, joy and love in our lives.

While I do agree with the fundamental principle that we are co-creators of our own lives, there is more to it than just visualizing and believing and then the life circumstance that you desire will appear. There is a bigger picture, and we must understand this bigger picture to truly grasp the meaning of life and, thus, the path to true and lasting happiness while we are here.

In 1999-2000 my life was in pretty bad rut. I was separated from my wife of 9 years and was in the process getting a divorce. I worked in R&D at a chemical company in a job that I was totally ill-suited for and I could barely bring myself to get through a day. At that time I decided that the solution to my problem was to quit my job, move to northern California and go back to school for an MBA and then start some new and exciting career with an up and coming dot com or maybe as a consultant. I had all of the right credentials to go to business school: a near perfect score on the GMAT standardized test, Bachelors and PhD degrees in chemical engineering, and 6 years of solid work experience at a Fortune 500 company. I figured that I was a shoe-in wherever I wanted to go.

I really wanted to go to business school at Stanford. It was one of the top ranked business schools in the nation, it was located where I wanted to be and I thought that it would fit me and my personality. It was around this time that I was first introduced to the concept of visualization and the Law of Attraction. So every day for months I wrote down my mantra that I would be accepted to Stanford Graduate School of Business with a full scholarship 25 times in the morning and 25 times at night. I fully believed that this was going to happen and it never even entered my mind that it wouldn't. So when I received my very polite letters declining me admission from Stanford and from Berkley too, I was absolutely devastated. I had locked in and focused so completely on one certain way for my life to proceed that when it evaporated I was left with no anchor.

So was this just a case of me not practicing my manifestation exercises proficiently or frequently enough? Not likely, I was so focused on going to Stanford that I could taste it. What this event and other similar ones that I have experienced since have shown me is that sometimes, no matter how much you visualize something, it is just not meant for you at that time. The conclusion that I came to was that there is a bigger plan in motion than what I think will make my life easier and more comfortable. So while I still believe that you create your own experience, I now realize that what I have is the ability to create my own inner experience and reactions to life. While I am able to influence my external circumstances with my thoughts and actions, I am not necessarily able to create every outer circumstance to fit my desires as I understand them. There is a larger design to the outer forces that impinge upon our lives. Realizing this fact and living as if everything that happens to us is for the purpose of helping us to realize our highest destiny in this lifetime is the key to accessing our natural state of joy and happiness.

Happiness is a Choice

Don't worry, be happy
-- Meher Baba via Bobby McFerrin

We all deserve to be happy. In fact, we are all born to be happy. Just look at babies and small children. Their natural state is smiling, laughing without a worry in the world. However, as we grow up and integrate into our respective cultures of daily living, we lose touch with this natural state of freedom and trust. But, even though we lose touch with our natural state of happiness it is not lost. We are able to regain our experience of living in complete and utter joy by reconnecting with this state.

I like to think of our choice to remain disconnected from our happiness in this way; it is as if we naturally live in the most beautiful, serene wonderful place that you can imagine, a literal Eden. However, we have tightly wrapped ourselves head to toe in a thick wool blanket so that we cannot see, hear, smell or taste the paradise where we live. All we experience is the darkness, stifling heat and claustrophobic condition created by this blanket. We only need to let the blanket go and it will fall off, revealing the ecstasy of our true state. However, we are terrified to let go of the blanket because it is all that we know and we are afraid that if we begin to let go of the blanket we will lose the little that we have. So the work of practicing happy is to gradually convince ourselves that it is ok to let go of the blanket and to let ourselves unwrap, bit by bit until we can clearly see that not only do we not need the blanket, but also once we drop it our existence is divine paradise.

Unfortunately, most of us do not believe that we have the ability to drop the blanket. Most of the people who I talk to blame their unhappiness on external circumstances. However, if we take a moment to think about it, it is clear that whether we choose to be happy or upset at a particular set of circumstances is all in our mind. For example, if I have been unemployed for two years and am barely able to live and then I receive a paycheck for $100,000 for me to work the next entire year, that would make me deliriously happy. However, if Donald Trump had to take the same deal of a $100,000 paycheck for a year's work this would be very disappointing to him and likely cause him to be unhappy. So clearly, how we react to a set of circumstances is completely determined by our own state of mind. The great news is that our mind, and how we view anything and everything that happens in life is the one thing that is completely in our control. That's not to say we do not have a set of very ingrained habits that we allow to control our reactions, but if we created these habits, then we can certainly change them. This is the essence of making happiness a choice, training our minds to a view of life that will serve us best.

My Intention with this Teaching

My underlying assumption throughout this work is that you already realize that you would rather be happy than unhappy; otherwise, you would probably not be reading this book. For much of my life I have lived "out of the flow", completely lost with no idea about the purpose of my life except knowing that I wasn't on the right track. I felt unfulfilled, frustrated and depressed. However, over a period of about twelve years I was given the gifts of the teachings and the life experiences that have allowed me to shift my state of mind from that of a fundamentally unhappy to person to one of a fundamentally happy person. This shift has completely changed my experience of life, allowed me to have much richer relationships with my wife, children and friends and allowed me to begin to live with a passion and zest for life that I never imagined was possible for me. I am so grateful for receiving these gifts that I am motivated to share what I have learned. I hope to offer others a road map to experience the same shift as I have in a way that takes less time and requires less bumps along the way. Therefore, my intention in writing this book is to share the experiences, practices and exercises that have helped me to move from a place of deep disconnect and depression to one where I experience deep joy and happiness on a daily basis. **Practicing Happy** is my story and I feel that I am meant to share what I have learned because breaking the bonds of unhappiness has been the most difficult challenge and yet the most fulfilling work of my life.

As with any information or teaching please take only those of my experiences and suggestions that resonate with you and leave anything else behind. I am not a perfect or completely enlightened being so don't take anything that I say as the word of gospel. There are certain fundamental truths that we discover, but the most important thing for this work is how to get on the path and then to start walking the path towards your self-realization. The practices in this book can provide a doorway to help you get in touch with your happiness. This does not mean that you will be completely free of pain and have only pleasurable experiences for the rest of your life. The entire range of emotions and experiences have their place and they all serve to remind us of how we are living. In fact, the most challenging and painful times in my life have taught me the most, moved me forward in my development and ultimately increased my ability to live the rest of my life in joy. Walking this path can help you to identify the underlying reasons for your experiences, and help you to maintain an inner peace as you work through them and work toward your ultimate freedom.

CHAPTER 2

WAKE UP!

You too can be happy

The happiness that I refer to in this book is the ultimate state of freedom and trust. Freedom from past conditioning that holds us in places, jobs and relationships that do not serve us. Trust to know that in each moment our lives are working out as they need to and that, by making choices in accordance with our inner guidance, we will live in a state of ease and joy.

We often associate the word happiness with strong feelings of well being, inner peace and harmony. Alternatively, one can experience feelings of anxiety, unease, aloneness, fear and confusion, which I will refer to as unhappiness. Most of my life I have felt stuck in a deep place of unhappiness. Much of this time I didn't even identify it as unhappiness as it was so normal to me that I couldn't imagine feeling a different way. In fact, when I would run across people who seemed to live in a place of ease, happiness and joy I convinced myself that chronically happy people were lacking in either intelligence or awareness of their true situation, because, if they were smart, then they would realize that they should be unhappy like me. The only time that I glimpsed what true happiness feels like are those times when I first fell in love or when I was really present and connected with my children. You know the feeling, the one when your entire body is alive and tingling at the thought of your beloved, your heart is full of joy and nothing else in life bothers or concerns you. That feeling is what we are all able to attain on a regular basis regardless of what else is going on in our lives.

The reason that I know that what I have learned is available to you is that I have not lived an extraordinary life. I didn't go to India to study under a guru and meditate for 30 years, I didn't wake up one morning as an enlightened being, and I was never struck by lightning. What led to my evolution was the combination of an exposure to a variety of spiritual teachings that completely transformed my view of the world and the various events and challenges of my life that served to drive home these teachings. Over a ten plus year period I was essentially in intensive training and I developed from depressed, hopeless, scared and full of negativity to strong, confident, happy and full of love. That's not to say that this has been an easy transformation. As with intense physical training, I was often presented with significant challenges and pushed to my limits. However, it was these exercises that led to my greatest improvement and growth. Also, like any training, it is up to you how fast and hard that you want to go. Some of us will travel a less strenuous slower paced route than others but as long as we are on the path together, we will see results and experience drastic changes in how we experience our lives.

The Meaning of life

If you do what you've always done, you'll get what you've always gotten
-- Anthony Robbins, Motivational Speaker and Self Help Guru

If you do not change direction, you may end up where you are heading.
-- Lao Tzu

The core reason why we don't experience happiness and fulfillment is that we don't understand the game of life and, as a result, we are playing it all wrong. While a great many of us consider ourselves spiritual or religious, we make all of our decisions as if everything that we see is all that there is. We are completely materialistic in that our lives are geared towards creating "material" success and we believe that our happiness will come from some specific set of conditions in the physical world such as financial abundance, the right romantic relationship, physical health, etc. However, that view is completely wrong.

We are truly spiritual beings having an experience as a body on earth. We all have a soul that "animates" our bodies and is the underlying source for who we are in our lives. Moreover, when our soul decided to be born into this world as a person, it did so with strong desires for what it would learn for its own evolution and what role it would play to help other souls evolve. The ultimate goal of all souls is to eventually "wake up". Therefore, each of us is a soul longing to fulfill its destiny and when we are living in sync with that longing happiness abounds and when we are out of sync then loneliness, anxiety and depression rule the day.

Unhappiness comes from the resistance – the not wanting – of things the way they are. This resistance comes from a basic misunderstanding of this life and the world. I have come to realize that my unhappiness was caused by the fact that I was out of touch with my true nature and my reason for being alive. It was this realization, along with a lot of help from others and personal practices to retrain my habitual ways of thinking that has resulted in me being able to live more in my happiness and to be able to be the husband, father, friend and co-worker that I truly want to be. While my feelings and emotional state can still vary throughout the day, much of the time I am at peace and filled with joy. If you are skeptical that this is possible, know that I used to feel the same way. I ask you to stay with me, listen to my story with an open heart and see if any of what I say works for you because, believe me, living in this state of being is so much better than how I used to live that it hardly seems like it was my life.

To begin this journey one of the first steps is for us to realize that maybe we don't already know everything that there is to know; to be conscious of the fact that what we take to be true about life and reality may be incomplete or even deeply flawed. Obviously, if you have a desire to be happier in your life than you currently are then something isn't working, and I am a true believer in the quote at the beginning of this section, "if you do what you've always done, you'll get what you always gotten." Thus, I invite you to explore and be open to new ideas and ways of thinking that may help you to experience the life that you want.

Any model of reality, much like Newton's equations that we learned in high school physics class, are just our best description of what we understand rather than the full complete truth of our universe. We can always try to find some piece of our experience that doesn't seem to fit into the model (like quantum effects in physics), but we don't throw out the entire system because it is still very useful for building houses, airplanes and computers and we can even send a man to the moon using them. Therefore, we should use any model of reality to help us to move forward and improve our experience of life and then as times come where we need more or have advanced beyond the limitations of our worldview we will then find and/or develop new ways of understanding that both incorporate and expand our current ways of thinking and continue to use that which is helpful to us and discard that which holds us back or takes us in the wrong direction. So I encourage you to take a deep look at how you currently view the world, consider the suggestions that I am making about the nature of our reality and then take what helps you to move forward and leave the rest behind.

An alternate worldview

The foundation of the practices that I propose in this book is a way of looking at the world and life that I have evolved to over the years. I was raised in a fairly traditional Christian (Lutheran) system of belief and went to school and worked as a chemical engineer so I was taught a very specific view of God, the physical world and how it all works. But, I never really learned anything about why we exist or what our purpose is. Over the years my experiences and subsequent study have broadened my view of life and the universe to one that has become very useful for my personal growth and happiness. So as far as this goes I agree with the philosophy that it is not useful to endlessly debate the correctness of a model of reality or try to justify every seeming exception to the rule. But if a world view works for you and helps you to grow then use it, and if it doesn't then let it go and move on.

Clearly there are unseen forces that we experience in our world. These include wind, waves that make music come out of our radios and even the energy that seems to animate a person's body while one is alive and then seems to leave when she dies. I will refer to the spark of energy that animates all living things as Spirit, and to the aspect of Spirit that identifies specifically to one person or being as soul or subconscious mind. You can substitute a term for Spirit that works for your belief system such as God, Christ, Holy Spirit, Tao, The One Mind, The Universe etc. In essence, we are all Spirit that has chosen to have the experience of living as a body in this world. Furthermore, the only reason that we chose to do this was so that we can learn and grow to awaken to our true nature, which is pure love. We have chosen to have this experience so that we may grow and evolve. The more that we are able to get in touch with our true nature then the more that we will be able to experience the true love that we are, the more joy and happiness that we will feel.

This view of the world clearly tells us that our life experiences are not rewards or punishment for our behavior, random occurrences or even the inevitable result of the physical and chemical forces put into motion at The Big Bang. Everything that we experience is specifically designed for us by our Spirit selves to help us to grow. Let me repeat that, EVERYTHING, every person, every situation, every difficulty, every opportunity exists only to help us to grow so that we can live in the blissful knowledge that we are true love – to be happy, and in fact, we planned all of this ourselves before being born.

So what does this mean? Well one thing is that our constant and total focus on the outcomes of what happens in our life is totally misguided. Our worth is not defined by whether or not our business made money, we got straight A's, or our marriage works . What matters is whether or not we learn what we need to learn from the situations that we experience and whether or not we are able to enjoy and not resist the process of learning. This shift in perception will free you and make an incredible difference in the quality of your life. The best part of all this is that this freedom is there for you and all you need to do is choose it. Choose your freedom.

While it is true that you only need to choose your freedom, I am not saying that it is necessarily an instantaneous or effortless process for everyone. The way that we currently think and react to situations in our life is deeply ingrained into our psyche and these are habits that take focus and effort to change. However, the great news is that Spirit is on our side and is constantly working to help us to learn and evolve to higher levels of being. I know that it can be done by anybody because I have done it and continue to do it (with a lot of help).

The path is laid out for you

The path is laid out for you by you. The whole reason that you are here is because this life is the best place for you to learn, grow and evolve the way you want to. An obvious question would then be, "If I am planning all of this for myself with the ultimate goal being happiness and joy, then why should I be experiencing pain and suffering?" The best answer to this is an analogy with physical training for a sport. Great athletes who reach their full potential design and execute strenuous workout regimens that can cause pain and discomfort as they stretch their bodies to their limits. Sometimes that which causes pain is necessary to facilitate our evolution to a higher state. Pain, tension and discomfort can be great teachers because they really get your attention. What is a more effective wake up call when you are in a deep sleep, a loud annoying alarm that you can't ignore or the rustling of a pleasant breeze through the trees? Both have their place, but both are necessary at different times to accomplish different things.

Why then is it necessary for us to learn from difficulties rather than from only the easy stuff? Our ultimate learning is that we need to stop believing that our experience of this physical world is our ultimate and true reality. If everything always went the way that we think we want it to go, then this would tend to reinforce our belief in this version of reality. That is why we designed our lives to have a mix of pleasure and pain, to help us to question what we see, to seek the higher meaning and, ultimately, learn, remember and wake up to who and what we truly are: magnificent, omnipotent creative spiritual beings. So how does it work?

Each time our soul decides to take on a new human lifetime it creates a 'Life Book' for that lifetime. That is, a predetermined script of the opportunities that it will have to learn the lessons that it wants to learn. In addition the plan includes how it will help others to learn the lessons that they want to learn. This is essentially a description of our destiny and purpose in this life along with a bunch of seeming outside events and circumstances that will help us to get there. For example, say as Spirit I decided that I needed to develop the ability to be strong in the face of criticism. I might imagine that I could learn this lesson best if in my lifetime I was forced to be a whistle blower at my company and have management attack me in a lawsuit. If I didn't completely learn the lesson from that experience it might then be helpful for my business partner to constantly attack my competence, ethics and fitness to take up space as a human being. Typically, I would tend to look at these events as me being the "victim" of these other people and just "bad luck" that they happened to me. With this point of view I would tend to foment a lot of anger at the other parties who seem to be causing me the trouble. However, if I realize instead that these people are actually not doing anything to me and this whole scene is a set up that I put into place for myself so that I can learn a lesson and heal old wounds then it is easier to have the experience without feeling anger, sadness or helplessness.

Since you have planned everything yourself, then really everyone you meet in life is you. The metaphor of a dream illustrates this point really well. One problem is that whenever you start talking about life as a dream, people think that you are saying that life doesn't matter. Nothing could be farther from the truth. Life is incredibly important, otherwise you wouldn't bother doing it. It is no less than a key step on the path to return to God. What we learn is real, how we grow and overcome our limitations is real, but most of the stuff that we identify with when we are here is not real.

As an illustration, consider the case where you fall asleep at night and have a dream. In that dream you are walking around, you may sit on a bench, climb a tree, talk to your best friend, have lunch with someone you don't know, etc. So, who exactly are the people who you are talking to in your dream? They are you, of course, because it is your mind who made up the scenarios, people and conversations. Essentially, you were just talking to yourself through what seemed to be other people. This is how our life experience is constructed. There is only one of us and that one is working toward removing all of its blocks, misunderstandings and limitations to return to its natural state of wholeness, unlimited creative power and pure unchanging bliss.

Keeping this in mind, we now have a sound basis for "forgiving" the people and events that seem to attack us or make our lives unpleasant. As a result, we do not carry with us the negative energy that normally would be created in these circumstances and we take significant steps forward. As we learn to become love consistent with our life plan, this will naturally keep us in the flow so that we can live in a deep sense of joy and peace.

The concept of a Life Book or of a life plan scripted before birth has often been a point of struggle for me and I know that it causes a lot of controversy and confusion for people who study this concept. The confusion usually takes a form similar to this: "If my life is already planned out in a script then why should I even try or do anything. This means that I do not create my own life and I am just at the mercy of the script." On the other hand, at the opposite end of the spectrum is the following view: "Without a divine hand in my life, then I am free to create any life and circumstances that I choose. However, how do I know what to choose and when things do not work out as I intended is that just a coincidence resulting from my flawed practice of attraction and manifesting?" As with many difficult concepts, I have found an answer that works well for me by bringing together the opposing points of view.

My current view is that we are experiencing a world in which all of the outside events and circumstances have been scripted (by us though). However, as we experience these events and circumstances, we still have complete free will about how we choose to think about and react to these experiences. If I choose to resist the experiences, keep myself separate from them and their purpose in my life and choose not to learn and grow from them but rather to increase my negative energy, anger and fear, then the script will move onto another experience designed to teach the same truth but in a more effective way than the last one. As a person with a lot of experience in this lifetime of ignoring and missing these learning opportunities, I can attest that when the script tries to teach a lesson previously ignored it raises the intensity of the experiences. For example, I have had a whole series of teachings in this lifetime around money. The learning opportunities started with me losing all of my savings in the dotcom stock crash. Unfortunately, I completely missed the lessons. Then a few years later I was fired from my job and could not find another one. I still blamed my previous employer and the job market and refused to look at myself or the opportunities in it for me. Then I wasn't able to pay my bills and lost all of my credit cards. Still not listening. Then I had my car repossessed - still resistant - had the utilities turned off for brief periods of time. I was still angry at the world, God and anything else that I could name outside of myself. Got my car repossessed again, this time with $30k worth of my temporary employer's video equipment in the back. Now it is starting to sink in. But, still not there yet. Have my family evicted from our house, I'm learning and looking deeply at myself. We magically find a great place to land and now the flow around money is slowly starting to come back. Though I am still challenged around this lesson, the more that I am able to act on this philosophy and to retrain my mind to look inside for opportunity rather than to attack outside at what seems to be the immediately causing my problems the shorter and easier these circumstances are for me and the happier I am. As I look back at this pattern now, I can say to myself, "Gee, it sure would have been nice to be able to learn this lesson back in 1999 rather than having to deal with all of the help that I needed to learn it in 2009." So in an attempt to learn from this, anytime I come upon a life situation that is uncomfortable for me, I continue to train my mind to look within, to see this as a gift that I have given to myself and find the beauty in it for myself. This way, I can skip over the most annoying and painful parts of the script and be able to enjoy, love and be happy through whatever comes my way.

The path laid out in our Life Book creates a flow for our life. As soul beings we have complete and total free will. So as each opportunity from our Life Book presents itself we always have a choice. If we choose to look for the beauty and gift in every situation and react in love and gratitude then we will move with the flow of our lives, grow and evolve as we intended and be able to access the peace, joy and bliss of our true nature. However, if in these situations we choose to resist the opportunity for growth by blaming others for our discomfort and reacting with anger and attack, then we will forever be swimming upstream against the flow of our lives and be stuck in loneliness, anger and depression. The choice is ours, and we can choose anew in each moment of our lives here on earth.

Be in the flow

> *Go with the flow, man!*
> *-- Common saying*

When we are in the flow we feel the satisfaction, ease and inner peace of knowing that we are doing what we are supposed to be doing. We are happy. In addition, we experience all sorts of seeming coincidences and synchronicities that support our work and purpose. This does not mean that life will always be easy or that we will not experience a variety of challenges and difficulties, for these may be the best way for us to continue to learn and grow. It just means that we will be completing all of these lessons from a place of stability, confidence and joy.

When we are out of the flow we feel confused, distracted, lonely, disconnected and afraid. Everything that we try to do falls apart, we feel like we are beating our heads against the proverbial brick wall. Being out of the flow is a painful experience, and can lead to all manner of ills, including depression and physical disease. Often times this pain leads us to want to become numb to life. Now a days there are no shortage of ways to numb ourselves to life.

As I was going through college and graduate school and my early work career I was clearly out of the flow in my life. I suffered from depression, felt directionless and felt no passion for my life or where it was heading.

During this time I completely stopped exercising and spent most of my free time overeating (pizza and ice cream were my staples), watching television and sleeping. Being from Philly, I became completely absorbed in the local sports franchises so much that my entire focus and moods would rise and fall with the fortunes of the teams, especially my beloved Eagles. So I became an overweight, depressed sports fanatic who listened to sports talk on the radio all day long to try to distract myself from the fact that I was a completely lost soul, unhappy and not wanting to deal with my life. This is an example of being out of the flow.

It can be as just as obvious when the flow is tending to take us in a certain direction. As my daughter, Lotus, was turning 4, my wife, Anni, and I were desperately trying to find a way for her to attend a Waldorf school. She had been accepted to our local Waldorf school, where my wife's son had previously attended, but I had just begun working in a temporary position after a year of virtually no income following the collapse of our baby food company and we didn't have the money for the deposit. By this time in my life I had been practicing happy and while on the surface, the situation seemed stressful, at a deeper level I had complete confidence that as long as I kept doing my best that she would end up the place that she needed to be. Right around this time, Anni was inspired to go to the website of another highly regarded Waldorf school in our area and she noticed that they were looking for a Finance Director. The job description matched very closely to the wide variety of business and finance work that I had done since getting my MBA as a consultant and small business owner and within a matter of weeks I had a permanent job with health insurance and Lotus was attending pre-school at a greatly reduced tuition. In this situation things fell into place so perfectly that it couldn't possibly have been a series of coincidences and I knew that I was supposed to take this job. This move was clearly following the flow of my Life Book.

However, most of my life before starting this practice and a good portion of it since has been lived outside of the flow or purposefully swimming against it. This way of living leads to intense feelings of isolation, loneliness, victimhood, anger, depression, pain and suffering. In this situation we will all have our individual preferred methods for dulling the pain and trying to ignore the obvious signs that we are out of sync with our life purpose. I am sure that if you take a close look at your life, you will be able to identify your methods and the times in your life when you escaped into them the most. Some of the most common are using drugs, alcohol, or television to escape reality and pass our lifetimes without truly addressing the root issue. In fact anything that we use to distract ourselves from our lives can fit this bill including: overeating, sex, sports, movies, living vicariously through your kids, politics, etc. I am not saying that any of these are not enjoyable activities or great to have in your life. However, when used to excess as a way to distract you from your troubles they become an impediment to focusing on the truly important reason that you were born and can cause you to waste your life. This misuse of your lifetime will cause you even more sadness and pain and reinforce the cycle. However, the point is not to beat ourselves up over using these coping techniques but to be able to identify those times when we are getting out of the flow and to be able to get back into the flow as quickly as possible.

So take a look at your current life situation and determine whether you are in your flow or not. You can use these questions to guide your inquiry.

How do you know if you are **NOT** in the flow?

- Do you feel a heaviness and lethargy about your being?
- Do you feel like you have to struggle to get anything accomplished in life?
- Do you feel confused and directionless?
- Do you feel scared?
- Do you complain a lot?
- Do you constantly think through negative scenarios for everything in your life?
- Do you assume the worst, and then follow through with thoughts and actions based on this scenario?
- Do you feel hopeless?
- Are you overly self-conscious, constantly worried about how others perceive you?
- Do you think that you lack creativity and not able to create art, write poetry or pursue other creative endeavors.

If you answer yes to many of the above questions then you are out of flow in your life.

How do you know if you **ARE** in the flow?

- Do you feel lightness about your being?
- Do you frequently feel intense joy and love?
- Are you passionate about your life?
- Are you slow to anger and quick to forgive?
- Are you patient and flexible?
- Do you float above the dramas of life?
- Are other people powerless to make you feel bad?
- Are you confident and comfortable greeting new people?
- Are you able to identify with everything and everyone that you meet?
- Are you able to express yourself in creative forms?

If you answer yes to many of the above questions then you are in flow in your life. If you determine that you are in your flow, have always been in your flow and never expect to be out of your flow, then you can stop here and give the book to someone you know who needs it. However, if you are interested in exploring simple but powerful ways to get into the flow of your life and stay there, then let's take a look at what has worked for me.

We are all energy

$E=mc^2$
-- *Albert Einstein*

The final key concept that I want to discuss before we get into the practicing part of this path, is the fact that our entire universe is made up of nothing but energy that appears and exists in all different forms. Albert Einstein popularized this discovery with his famous equation $E = mc^2$. He showed mathematically that mass and energy are equivalent and can be transformed back and forth between the two states. This means that everything that we see, feel, taste, smell and hear is pure energy.

Obviously there are different qualities of energy that we perceive. For example, a rock is different from a plant, which is different from an animal, which is different from a human being, which is different from pure spirit. Many people refer to this difference in energetic quality as an entity's vibrational level. That is, someone or something with a low vibrational level has a lower intensity of energy and something with a high vibrational level has a higher intensity of energy. Typically, we would refer to dense matter such as rocks as having a lower vibrational level and a highly evolved spiritual being as having a high vibrational level. Similarly, emotions and feelings associated with separation, such as fear, anger, anxiety, and depression are considered lower vibrational energies and those associated with wholeness, such as love, happiness and peace are higher vibration.

One very important application of this concept relates to us being able to tap into the help that we need to progress on our journey from separation to wholeness. We are bombarded with constant communication from Spirit. Whether you view the source of this communication as the voice of God, the Holy Spirit, your higher self, or spirit guides this is where we need to go for help in staying in the flow of our lives. The trick to receiving this communication is for us to be in tune with the frequency of Spirit. I think of this like the radio in your car. When you drive you are swimming in a sea of radio waves that carry all types of information: news, music, talk shows, sports, weather, traffic etc. However, each source of information is broadcasting at a different frequency. The way that we are able to isolate and listen to any one of these sources is to tune our radio's frequency to that of the broadcast. In the case of receiving help from Spirit, we need to tune our minds to the frequency of spirit and quiet our thoughts so that we can hear what is being broadcast. For most of us, this means raising our level of energetic vibration from where we are today and practicing meditation or prayer to reach a place of receptive quiet. Any time you feel confused, alone and not knowing what to do, this is because you are not tuned into the frequency of spirit.

This energetic view of the world and ourselves is crucial not only to figuring out how to receive the guidance that we want and need, but also to deciding what methods will work best to help us grow. There are 4 basic levels at which we can perceive ourselves: (1) the physical level, where we see ourselves as physical bodies (2) the level of the mind, where we view ourselves through an intellectual lens, (3) the level of the soul, where we view ourselves as a separated spirit identified with this one body (this could be also called the subconscious mind) and (4) the level of pure spirit, where we realize that we are all one with the one Spirit and at this level there are no limitations or barriers. We mainly live in awareness of the first two levels and, at times, think in terms of the third and rarely, if ever, view life through the lens of the fourth.

The practical implication for this is that as we consider making changes in our lives we will look at different techniques that span the three levels of perception (at the fourth level, total oneness, there is no perception because as one whole, there is no other to perceive). For example, if we try to make changes only at the physical level, then there is no way that we can heal suffering at the level of the mind (thus psychotherapy was invented). Likewise, if you are addressing issues at the level of the mind, but the source of the problem is at the level of the soul, then you would not be able to truly heal or make lasting significant change unless you make changes at that level of energy. While there is no such thing as a problem or issue at the level of pure Spirit, if you can act in concert with that energy flow, then you will be able to move mountains without effort.

CHAPTER 3

THE SIMPLE CHOICE

Love or Fear; Wholeness or Separation

There is only one way to regain our true joy and happiness: to recognize, embrace and live in the knowledge that there is more to us than meets the eye. Even though what we see, hear, taste and smell suggests that we are all only bodies, we must remember that we actually are souls who have come to this life with intentions and a destiny to fulfill, and our bodies are nothing more than tools that we use along the way. Our key job is to live in concert with our soul's purpose

The difference between happiness and unhappiness in all of their forms comes down to a very simple choice. In every moment of every day you are either choosing love or choosing fear. These feelings are like light and dark in that when the light is on everything is illuminated and dark can only occur in the absence of light. Similarly, fear can only occur in the absence of love. So as we re-learn how to be and express only love, all fear will dissolve from our lives and we will be left in a state of pure joy and bliss. What could be better?

So many of us have lost the joy from our lives. We have been beaten down by crazy schedules, taking care of kids, energy-sucking jobs, financial challenges and health problems. However, the good news is there is a way to reconnect with our joy that doesn't require immediate resolution of all of our problems. We can build up an immunity to outside challenges by shifting our view of these things and opening up space to allow the laughter and joy back into our lives.

The Continuum

One simple way to look at the relationship between separation and wholeness, and how it relates to love, fear and happiness is to consider a continuum of world views that ranges at one end from seeing everything as one whole that is interconnected (we are all on the same team) to the other extreme of seeing everything as separate pieces that are disconnected from each other and only interact when they actually bump into each other (every man for himself). The figure below represents this continuum in thought system between wholeness/interconnectedness and separation/disconnectedness. The bottom part of the figure shows the corresponding experiences and feelings associated with these thought systems.

Most of us are living our lives near the far right extreme of this scale. We see ourselves as bodies, separate from all of the other people, animals, plants and rocks that we see in this world. We are completely absorbed in our own thoughts, problems, successes and failures and, while we are aware of the joys and pains of some of the other bodies, their challenges never seem to us as important as are our own.

Alternatively, spiritual masters such as Jesus, Buddha and Amma, to name a few, live their lives on the left end of this scale. They express divine love and compassion for everyone and everything, and teach that we are all one and that we should see ourselves (and them) in everything that exists. These masters live in a constant state of joy and peace and they demonstrate for us how it can be done. The evolution of how I look at myself and the world from complete separation to where I am able to see the threads that connect me with everything has shifted my experience of life in a profound way for the better. I am now much more happy, enthusiastic and passionate about my life where for as long as I can remember I carried a heaviness around with me that kept me weighted down and sad. I now feel a freedom to live, love and laugh. I am open to new people and experiences and feel a passion for life that is new to me. I enjoy playing with my kids more, have rejuvenated relationships with friends and family and draw new people and experiences into my life that have so enriched my experiences. I cannot overemphasize the change in experience of life that results from the shift of perception to the left on the Happy Curve. Even though I still fall back into my old views and habits from time to time, I now have the tools to recognize that these negative feelings are not normal or necessary and I am able to pull myself up and move back into my joy again.

However, as I said above in the introduction, don't just take my word for it. Compare what I am saying to your own life experiences. Look back at those times in your life when you have felt the absolute pinnacle of happiness and joy. Those times that you wish you could bottle the feeling

the happy curve

wholeness   *separation*

Love	Fear
Happiness	Unhappiness
Peace	Conflict
Trust	Anxiety
Forgiveness	Revenge
Beauty	Ugliness
Compassion	Anger/Attack
Reality	Illusion

and keep it with you always. For most people they are times when they felt intense love for another, the birth of a child, falling in love for the first time, being in the presence of intense natural beauty. These are all situations where we feel a deep connection with others and our surroundings. When in the presence of the awesome beauty and power of nature we feel at one with the universe. With other people these feelings of intense love give us the perspective of being joined with that person. When you love another deeply you are able to consider their needs along with or even above your own. In addition, look at how we express love to another: holding hands, hugging, kissing. These are all symbolic of joining with the other person, diminishing or outright destroying the separation between us. It is no coincidence that the ultimate representation of union, sexual intercourse, is also called 'making love'. The institution of marriage is the same way. When we love another person deeply and fully enough we go through a ritual that represents joining with that person so that where there were two separate entities now there is only one. So what if we were able to take the feelings of love and joy that we get from expressing love to those who we consider 'special' to us and express them to every person and all of creation with that same intensity. Think of the joy and happiness that we would experience. For the moment, let all of your judgments drop about whether this is possible or whether it is possible for you. Just consider the potential reward of traveling down this path. Isn't it worth giving it a try?

Cycle of Unhappiness

The challenge in moving towards the left of the Happy Curve is to break out of the self-reinforcing cycle of life that I call the Cycle of Unhappiness. Starting with our earliest childhood experiences we are taught that our happiness depends on outside factors. Therefore, there are sets of conditions that are "good" and sets of conditions that are "bad" and that we should be unhappy when bad conditions occur. Since unhappiness is a form of pain, we do everything possible to suppress, avoid or destroy those conditions that we perceive are causing the pain. This is much like the way we automatically slap at a mosquito that is biting our arm. It is the resistance to and attack of these circumstances that is the root of our problem and that traps us deeper in our anger and frustration. I invite you to consider the steps of the cycle on the next page.

The one place in this cycle where we have control and are able to make a choice is the decision in how we choose to perceive and react to the events and circumstances that present themselves in our life. Once we have made the choice that an event in our life is bad and contributes to our unhappiness, then the cycle is reinforced and continues to spiral. However, any time that we make the different choice that an event not only doesn't have control over how feel, but also brings to us a gift that we desperately need, we break the cycle, put ourselves into the flow and gain access to inner peace and joy. Regardless of what you have been taught, you do have the power to make this choice. All you need to create a new habit is to practice. Start today with the very next thing that you experience!

Choosing love in every moment

Only the soul that loves is happy.
-- Goethe

Love, love, love, that's what it's all about...
-- Song I used to sing in Sunday School as a child

cycle of unhappiness

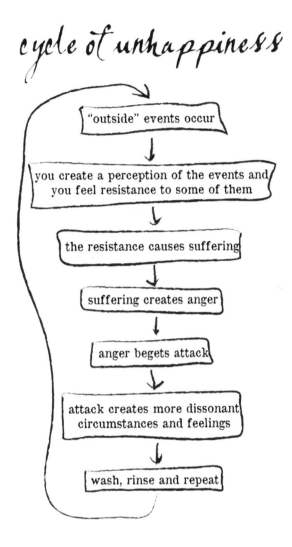

"outside" events occur

↓

you create a perception of the events and you feel resistance to some of them

↓

the resistance causes suffering

↓

suffering creates anger

↓

anger begets attack

↓

attack creates more dissonant circumstances and feelings

↓

wash, rinse and repeat

Every thought and resulting action that we have has its origin in either love or fear, there is no other possibility. Love leads to freedom, wellbeing and happiness and keeps you in your flow while fear leads to anger, resentment, anxiety and unhappiness. Love is our true nature and is the domain of Spirit while fear is of and for the benefit of our ego. We need to begin by using the Happiness Curve and taking a look at which side of the curve we are choosing with every thought, word and deed. Always choose love in any and all of its manifestations.

Love is primal and proactive. It is the most powerful force in our universe and is the core of what we are. When we are thinking and acting out of love, we are creating a positive space and environment for our lives to unfold. It inspires us to act out of generosity and empathy. Acting out of love is contagious and the more that you give, the more that you find you will receive in return. This is a self-reinforcing cycle that puts you in sync with your purpose and will bring you those things that you need to move toward living your purpose.

The problem with separation, on the other hand, is that it causes you to think of yourself and that which you desire (God, Christ, money, love, beauty, etc) as separate entities. This makes these things objects or states to be pursued, obtained and worshipped. However, in truth, you are love, you are prosperity, you are beauty, you are Christ, and you are God - you just need to stop thinking that you aren't. The mantra of separation, "If I get (fill in the blank here) then I will be happy," is so destructive because it not only has you chasing things that you will never find outside of yourself, but also creates the mindset of outside entities that have power over you (the power to deprive or hurt you) and thus, are to be feared.

Fear is a very powerful emotion and, thus, can be very destructive and limiting in our lives. I am not talking about the type of fear that discourages you from jumping into the Tiger pit when you visit the zoo. I'm talking about the fear that separates you from others and that prevents you from creating from your heart or pursuing your passion. Fear is simply the lack of light – it is always of the unknown and always of the other. It is the lack of knowledge of what has not happened yet. Some examples of these are fear of rejection, fear of being different, fear of change, fear of the unfamiliar and, of course, fear of loss of security. These fears are illusions; they are powerful aversions to things that have not happened and may not happen. Your fears are designed by your ego to keep you separate from others and from the path that will lead you to wholeness. Truly this type of fear has never stopped an unpleasant thing from happening. However, the fear does fill us with beliefs about what we cannot do and these beliefs keep us trapped and unable to move toward our passion and destiny. Fear gives rise to two major modes of self-preservation in the face of that which you are afraid of: Anger/Attack and Retreat/Withdrawal.

Anger is raw and reactive. It reveals a part of your emotional body or psyche that is painfully exposed and is reacting to a negative stimulus. Anger is a violent reaction to things not being as we think they should be. It is therefore ego based as we are again looking outside of ourselves for a source of happiness and peace. Anger also leads to attack, which is an offensive strategy that we use to try to force outside people and situations to be how we want them to be. We only attack when we are angry. Often, attack is such an ingrained response that, when anger rises, we attack whomever or whatever is close by even if they have nothing to do with that which we think is actually the source of our pain. The long lasting damage of anger is that it creates highly focused negative energies that we carry with us until they are healed. Without healing and release, these energies reside within our bodies to be constantly brought up and experienced again and again.

The other major mode of self-preservation in the face of fear is retreat and withdrawal. This is a defensive measure and also represents a type of resistance that can come in two forms. The first is to build a shell around you so that you don't let anything in at all that could hurt you. This not only blocks out all love, but also prevents anything in that could disappoint you. The other form of this defense manifests by numbing yourself to all outside stimulus. We do this with drugs, alcohol, television, extreme sports, etc. That is not to say that any of these diversions are bad in and of themselves, but they can be used to cut you off from the world as a way to pass the time without really experiencing your life.

An example of this in my life occurred back in my mid-20's I became so filled with fear that I would never want to go out to an unfamiliar place – even to do things that I enjoyed. I was living in the East Bay outside of San Francisco and I loved great food and great wine. However, I was absolutely terrified of the thought of driving into downtown San Francisco to try the great restaurants that were so close by. The main source of my fear was that I wouldn't be able to get into the right lane or find a way to park without doing something "wrong", having someone honk or yell at me or something like that. Of course it was absolutely ridiculous, but it paralyzed me to the point of fighting tooth and nail against going to do something that I actually really enjoyed. So this fear, in all of the ways that it manifested, not only kept me away from experiencing something that I enjoyed but also seriously damaged my relationship with my spouse. At some point, after a divorce was inevitable I finally woke up. A simple question to me triggered a complete release of my self-limiting thoughts in this respect and I started to choose to not let what other people might think of me control my life. Nothing more was necessary to completely change my life than to choose a different thought pattern.

In each moment with each twist and turn of our life, we get another opportunity to choose love vs. fear, wholeness vs. separation, beauty vs. ugliness, forgiveness vs. revenge, etc. Make a copy of the Happiness Curve and put it on your bulletin board, tape it to your bathroom mirror and commit it to memory. That way you can become vigilant about paying attention to the choices that you make and choosing your reactions rather than staying a slave to your current habits.

Find the Beauty

"Beauty is truth, truth beauty," - that is all
Ye know on earth, and all ye need to know.
-- John Keats from Ode on a Grecian Urn

You will notice that beauty is a descriptor on the happy side of the Happy Curve. The perception and expression of beauty is one of the ways that we are hardwired from birth to recognize Truth when we see it. Beauty marks the sign posts that guide us toward our passion and bliss. Since we inherently recognize those things that we find beautiful and those that we don't, beauty provides us with an easy system to help guide our choices through life.

Every time that you are presented with a choice in life, ask yourself, Is what I am doing beautiful?" If your first reaction is yes, then go forward with love and passion. However, if your first reaction is no, then this is an incorrect choice and it will take you farther away from where you want to be, so stop and change your approach. Here are some examples of common choices that we make every day:

Truth is beautiful
Lies are ugly

Sincerity is beautiful
Sarcasm is ugly

Love is beautiful
Fear is ugly

Wholeness is beautiful
Separation is ugly

Compassion is beautiful
Hate is ugly

Infuse everything that you do in a day with beauty. If you are creating beauty then you are doing the right thing no matter what anyone else is telling you. One of the themes throughout this book is that everything that happens in your life is a gift given to you by you. So find the beauty in everything that happens, revel in it and express it back out into the world.

All that you have to give in the world is your creativity. If you create beauty, in all of its forms, then you are following your path and fulfilling your purpose. This is all that you can control and all that you have come here to do. Don't ask for advice, don't judge what you've created by whether it makes money, is popular or even whether or not it works as intended. Take any pain or attacks that you receive and turn them into beauty.

So use beauty to help you find your way, see the beauty in everything and turn everything into beauty. Failing to express beauty and goodness is as much a block to your progression as is expressing ugliness and evil. Become the artist that you are meant to be with the world as your canvas. Beauty is all you need.

CHAPTER 4

CHANGE THE SOFTWARE

Reactive vs. conscious living

We now have our goal. We are aiming to move our world view from one of a bunch of separate beings randomly bumping into each other to one of wholeness, where everyone and everything is interconnected all working together in concert, much like all of the cells in our body work in concert to create a healthy organism. As we set the stage for the work to be done, there is one key concept that we must wrap our minds around in order to Practice Happy. This is the fact that our happiness is completely within our own control. Our happiness does not depend on outside circumstances, how other people act or what occurs in our life. No matter what else happens, we can choose our reaction and we can make the choice of how we want to feel. So all we have to do is to choose to be happy, it is very simple, though it can be quite a challenge at first.

Unfortunately, right now, most of us have not taken control of our lives. How we think, how we feel, and how we react have all become completely automatic and seemingly out of our control. It is as if we were trained from birth that when we see a red bird we slap ourselves across the face. This habit becomes so entrained that we don't notice the mechanics of what is happening, but we do notice that whenever we see a red bird our face hurts. Given this understanding of the situation we of course blame the red bird for our pain and now we hate red birds. However, what if someone explained to us that the red bird was not doing anything to us, but its presence just triggered a learned response of slapping ourselves in the face, so that we are actually the one causing our own pain. Once we realized this, then we could start to break the habit of slapping ourselves whenever we see a red bird and eventually the sight of a red bird would not trigger any reaction at all and we could finally see and appreciate the bird for what it truly is.

The concept that you can choose your thoughts and, as a result, are in complete control of your happiness is a foreign one to most of us and is certainly not taught by our culture at large. Whether we realize it or not, we are programmed with a thought system that believes that how we feel is completely controlled by the events and conditions that come from outside of us. That is, in order to be happy we have to meet certain conditions in our life such as: financial success, a romantic relationship, the respect of our peers, a healthy, attractive body, etc. How many people do you know are able to have all of these conditions lined up at the same time all of the time? Also, what about the people who seem to have it all and yet still aren't happy? It doesn't take much examination to conclude that our basic paradigm about happiness doesn't work. So why not try something else?

Driving my car parable

One day I was driving my car in traffic in Santa Monica, CA and the car behind me honked its horn. I immediately assumed that the person was honking at me, which brought up feelings of anger and resentment. I reacted to these feelings by making an obscene gesture towards the other driver and purposely slowing down in an attempt to annoy them. I carried these feelings of anxiety and resentment with me for several hours until I eventually forgot about the incident. This was not one of my best moments, but it does demonstrate a reactive tendency that I have often displayed.

In this example there are two factors that prevented me from staying peaceful and happy: (1) the subconscious programming that told me that the honking was criticism and should make me feel bad and (2) the fact that my feelings and actions all ran on a sort of autopilot without my conscious examination. As I reacted to the honking horn I did not make any of these decisions consciously. I didn't stop and say to myself, gosh, I should interpret the horn honking as a criticism directed towards my driving skills, then I will choose to feel angry and resentful in this situation and I will follow it all up by trying to attack back at what I perceive as the source of the criticism. If my goal is happiness then, obviously, I would not have consciously chosen this path because anger and attack clearly do not make me good or happy.

So why did I react that way then? Clearly I was not in conscious control of my reactions but was a "victim" of the unconscious habits that I have built up to protect my sense of self. My sensitivity to criticism stems from the thought that if somebody was criticizing me, then that must mean that I am flawed and inferior. Following this logic, I must constantly be on the lookout for anything that could be interpreted as a criticism and I must immediately and completely refute any validity of the perceived criticism. Furthermore, I must fiercely attack the source to discourage further criticism, especially if I feel that the criticism has some validity. Even though this may sound crazy, it is the natural, logical defense mechanism for a psyche that thinks it can be harmed by outside criticism. We will come to see that this is the fundamental flaw. Criticism, valid or not, cannot hurt us unless we choose to be hurt by it. The choice to be hurt by and to react to attack or criticism of any kind is just a habit that we have deeply ingrained in our psyche.

To break this cycle that leads to stress, anxiety, and unhappiness, we must turn off the autopilot so that we become conscious in the moment when the feelings arise, and then choose how we want to react, both internally and outwardly in every situation. In addition, we must reprogram our psyche to realize that we are invincible and can only be hurt by people, situations or events if we choose to be.

When I say that we are invincible, I mean that even though we see ourselves as psychologically and physically frail physical beings, that is not who we truly are. We are pure spirit. Our lives here on earth are akin to the concepts presented in the movie The Matrix. In that movie, the hero, Neo, realizes that what he thought was his life was actually all taking place in his mind, like a dream. So in truth, his body, other people, the entire physical world he saw did not actually exist outside of an illusion, a very realistic dream, that he was having. This being the case, Neo was able to learn that even though he was having certain experiences in the illusion, what seemed to be happening to him could only limit or hurt him if he believed that they could. Similarly, our spirit, or soul, is aware of all the experiences that we are having here and is able to learn and evolve based on those experiences, but in the end, it is all just an illusion and nothing that happens here on earth can hurt or destroy our soul. In the end, when our body is destroyed, killed or just laid aside, we wake up to our true nature and realize that we were safe at home the entire time. So as long as we can keep the proper perspective about our true nature and realize that we are experiencing a grand play put on for our own personal benefit, then it becomes easy to live through difficult experiences without feeling like we need to beat ourselves up or attack other people in order to protect your "status" as perfect (whatever that means). Hey, we all make errors in our lives, otherwise, there wouldn't be any point for us to be here. So if we look at everything as part of our grand plan to grow towards that state of endless pure joy and ecstasy, it gives us a stronger base to make that bill collector, repo man, disease or annoying driver honking his horn look more like a gift and less like a reason to stress.

So back to my example. If my goal were happiness in the honking situation then it would have been helpful if I would have consciously observed the feelings that were arising and then interrupted the cycle of habitually determined reaction. If I had chosen to react in love and compassion rather than in anger and attack then I could have interpreted the honk of the horn not as a criticism of me but as a request for help. If I had chosen to try to see if there was something that I could do to help the other driver and rather than attack him reached out in pure love to him, even if only with a kind thought, then my response would have left me feeling peaceful and happy as I continued on my way. So our key task in learning to practice happy will be to learn to choose our reactions to life's situations differently. Any change, especially change of deeply ingrained habits, is not easy. However, it is achievable with a strong desire to do so and the discipline to keep practicing, especially in the challenging moments.

A few weeks later, I was driving in my car again, and a person honked their horn at me again. The same initial feelings of anger and annoyance rose up in me, but this time I was aware that this was happening. Instead of reacting angrily, I became consciously aware of my feelings and decided that I was not going to let a honking horn control how I felt. After a few minutes of deep breathing, I was able to let go of the feelings and the incident was a big improvement over my previous experience. Over time, in similar situations those feelings of anger and resentment don't even arise so I do not usually become upset. All it takes is the intention to be conscious of my reactions, to question my ingrained assumptions about how I want to react, and then plenty of practice. My experience has been that if you provide the first two, this world will give you plenty of opportunities to practice. In fact, as a side note, be careful what you ask for. I remember a few days when I would wake up feeling great and strong and would make the commitment to myself that I would practice conscious living and forgive everything that would happen in the upcoming day. Without fail, Spirit would throw me a few real doosies that day (like getting a car repossessed). At the time I interpreted this phenomena as every time I started to feel good, the Universe was trying to knock me back down, but in retrospect I can see that working with the more challenging situations is what helped me to grow the fastest and was a great gift to me.

Competitiveness

The ego is the source of all of our discomfort and unhappiness. At its core, the ego is our sense of individuality, of separateness from each other. As such, for it to exist the ego must justify itself as a separate being. If we can't come up with a good reason why we deserve to be here, to be a separate person from everyone else, then maybe we shouldn't be here at all.

This is the root cause for constantly comparing ourselves to others and to our egos' ideas for what makes a successful person. This thought system is also the source of the discomfort, hurt and unhappiness that results when we do not fare well in these comparisons.

My wife, Anni, and I started a baby food company in 2005 called Bohemian Baby. We loved this company, its employees, its customers and its mission in the world. However, after two and a half years, through a series of seemingly unfortunate events around the funding of the company it died a slow and painful death. We had sunk every penny that we had and many that we didn't have into trying to resuscitate the company as it went down and its final collapse left our financial and work lives in a complete shambles.

A few years later we came across some news stories of a couple whom we had met during the Bohemian Baby days and had come close to teaming up with to bring out a new line of products under the Bohemian Baby name. Unfortunately, these discussions came as the company began to collapse and I was distracted and the relationship ended on a sour note. Anyway, it seems that this couple had then invested their resources in a different product and had been able to build what seemed like a very financially successful business in a very quick manner.

As we looked at the different paths our businesses had taken Anni and I could not help, despite our best efforts, to feel anger and frustration. Why had our incredible efforts gone down the tubes while this other couples' had blossomed into success? Why did I have the deep in my gut feeling that I had failed while they had succeeded? At that time I could intellectually tick off all of the key points that I am making in this book: (1) it is not about specific outcomes but what we learn in the process (2) the events of all of our lives are perfectly orchestrated so that we learned what we needed to learn and they learned what they needed to learn (3) their financial success and our lack thereof were not indicators of their superior worth as human beings and our inferiority, etc. However, for a few hours I was still experiencing that gnawing feeling of angst, which was keeping me from being in my full happiness.

This nagging feeling was a signal to me that my ego still held significant sway over me on this issue. I still had the habit of intrinsically defining success and worth based on which outcome most fed my ego and justified my existence as an individual, in this case that was the business and financial success that is so valued in our culture. Even though I could clearly see the incredibly important and affirming learnings and growth that I took from the difficult path that Bohemian Baby traveled, and I could even see the important role that Anni and I played in inspiring that couple to take a leap into action on their business ideas and that all of the events played out perfectly to propel us down our current path and them down theirs, I still had some of the old habit energy in there.

In the end, I now realize that I only have need for competition when I do not have a strong belief in myself. Competition is actually a way that I define my own worth when I am not sure if I am worthy or not. It provides some measure, no matter how flawed, of my value as a human being. I have found that the more that I have been able to internalize the worldview that this life and what I accomplish doesn't define me and that my success as a human depends only on how I evolve and grow and work towards fulfilling the destiny that I long for the less need I have for competition and the less that comparison of myself to others affects me.

As you travel down this path and become more aware of the negative feelings that you engender by comparing yourself to others, I do have a suggestion that has been invaluable to me as I transcend these old patterns. One of the most helpful concepts for me that I took from the book **A Course In Miracles** is that in this entire learning process we all experience thousands upon thousands of lifetimes, and over these lifetimes we play every role that there is to play. We have been the oppressors, we have been the oppressed, we have been rich and poor, strong and weak, smart and dim. So whenever I find myself in a challenging situation where my ego tends to want to make me feel badly about myself, I remember that the fact that I find myself in financial lack does not make me a flawed person, it is just my time now to have this experience for a specific learning to occur and I have been rich in the past and will be rich again in the future before this is all over. This mindset has really helped me in many situations where I was getting down on myself for the situation that I was in at a particular moment in time. As for the example above, this particular concept got me most of the way and my realization that coming across this information was a gift from Spirit to inspire me to write this section of this book is what allowed me to completely release all negativity around it and really feel love and joy towards the other couple, towards myself and be grateful for how everything has and continues to work out.

If outcome doesn't matter then why do anything?

This is a question that I have struggled with and heard many times during my spiritual studies. The ego holds onto focusing on outcomes very tightly because, once you let go of outcomes and focus on enjoying the process of learning and growth, you move away from focusing only on your individual self and more towards the collective - away from ego consciousness and towards unity consciousness where the pure bliss of God resides.

When we say that focus on outcomes is not important, what we mean to say is that focus on outcomes at the level of physical form is not the point of your life and will forever lead to unhappiness as you cannot control outcomes on that level. The true outcomes of our life events are the learning and healing that come along with them. These happen at the level of the mind and we do have complete control over what we choose to learn and what we choose to ignore. So while we live here it is inevitable that we will do stuff and we will work to accomplish specific goals on the level of form. However unless we learn to not be attached to the outcomes on this level we will not be able to transcend suffering and live in joy. As with everything that I am talking about here, we are all practicing and learning which is why the book is not called Perfected Happiness. We must always remember to be compassionate with ourselves and others and not be too hard on ourselves when we fall back into old habits. They key is to realize what we are doing and continually trying to do better.

As we focus on staying in the flow of our lives, our tasks and roles that we need to take on to further our own and others' growth will become clear. However, we must always remember that sometimes, not achieving the outcome that we want to accomplish is exactly the lesson that we need. Life is like a dance. The purpose of dancing is the experience of it, not whether or not we end up at a specific point on the floor at the end. So learn to enjoy the process of life because if we only focus on what we think the outcomes of our efforts should be, we will end up missing the entire point of why we chose to be born.

There is help for you

There will be times when you feel like the entire world is against you. The people who you are closest to, the ones who you count on the most will attack you and you will feel completely and utterly alone – an unwelcome stranger in your own home. Even in these times you are completely surrounded by help and support from Spirit and your own higher self. These spiritual beings are constantly beaming helpful information, love and light to you so that even in the tough times, you feel supported and can find and keep your center.

We are constantly being sent information and guidance from Spirit. We just need to develop the sensory ability to perceive it regularly and reliably. The most common form of receiving this communication when we are tuned in is in the form of feeling or intuition. This help also comes as ideas, inspiration or flashes of insight. During the writing of this book the times when I was most open I received the content almost as dictation from my subconscious. The words just flowed out of my mind.

People have also reported receiving information from Spirit through visions, dreams, conversations with spirit guides and even by channeling Spirit into this world. However it happens for you, getting in touch with Spirit through one or more of these methods is critical support that you need in the process of remembering why you are here and accessing the help you need.

Practice makes perfect

Now that we have an idea of what we want to accomplish (moving from separation to wholeness, from fear to love, from unhappiness to happiness) and we have a general framework for viewing life and the world that will help us to make that shift, the question remains how do we go about actually doing it? I know that for me it was very different to say that I want to be happy than it was for me to actually be at a place where I was happy. This is no different than the difference for many of us between saying that we want to lose weight, we want to eat better, we want to plant a garden or we want to stop smoking and actually doing it. The reason for this challenge in every case is habit.

Habit is the force that tends to keep us doing what we have always done rather than doing something different. It is a momentum that takes a certain amount of work and energy to break and, depending on how deeply ingrained the habit is, it can take a lot of work and effort in order to break it. However, the good news is that every habit can be broken, and no matter what pattern of thinking or doing is keeping you trapped in an experience of reality that you don't like, someone out there has already escaped from it.

CHAPTER 5

THE PATH

There is no way to happiness; happiness is the way.
  -- The Buddha

The path is not the destination. Any thought system that you use to move towards enlightenment will not, by definition, be enlightened. This is because the thought system is part of the world of duality and separation and not of the wholeness of enlightenment. The path is just a tool to help you get from your point of departure to your destination. For example, if I take the freeway from my house to the beach, the freeway is not the beach. The freeway guides me in the right direction and is there to keep me from getting off track, but once I get to the beach, I must leave the freeway behind. It has served its purpose for me and if I cling to it, I will never be able to fully enter the beach or enjoy the sand and ocean and that I am seeking. Just as being on the freeway will never actually be playing at the beach, being on the path to enlightenment will never fully be enlightenment.

So do not get too attached to your path or assume that this or any path that works for you is the one true way to the beach. The freeway works great if you have a car and live close to an entrance ramp. But, if you don't have a car, stop trying to take the freeway and hop on a train, or walk, or crawl if you have to, but just keep moving, no matter what.

Go into training

There are only two mistakes one can make along the road to Truth: not going all the way, and not starting.
-- Buddha

When attempting to accomplish anything in life, it can help to think in terms of training to meet the challenge. For example, if my goal is to run a marathon I don't expect to be able to sit on my couch for the next 6 months eating potato chips and watching television (even if I'm watching people run on television!) and then have the capacity to go out and run a marathon. I know that it will take time and effort to transform my body from where it is today into one that has the ability to complete this task. Furthermore, I know that I need to create a workout regimen for myself that will foster and support this transformation. So this is what we are doing in this book. We are creating a Happiness Workout.

Underlying this workout are seven techniques that have made it possible for me to make the changes necessary to drastically improve my life. In my case, these seven did not come naturally and I had to learn them and to make them habit. Even after I learned them in my head it took me quite a bit of effort and practice to integrate them into my body and unconscious mind to allow me to make significant progress and take me out of depression and into happiness. These principles are: (1) Intend it (focus) (2) Take action (GOYA) (3) Be disciplined (4) Be a warrior (relentless, adaptive) (5) Integrate (6) Purify, and (7) Practice, practice, practice.

Intend it!

Where attention goes, energy flows.
---A saying that I saw on a T-shirt once

The power of intention is gaining more awareness in our culture through various programs and books that tell us how to manifest things in our lives. Many of these teachings say that we can have anything we want in the world if we visualize ourselves having it. My experience tells me that while I have been able to manifest many things in my life with strong intentions, not everything goes as I intend it. This is because before I was born I set out a very strong set of intentions for what I wanted to learn and do in this life. At times these pre-birth intentions may come into conflict with my desires here and often the intentions that I put out as spirit will have more strength than those that I put out once I am here.

For example, when I decided that I wanted to go to business school at Stanford it was out of a sense of ego. I wanted the status of attending a top school and I wanted to be able to easily get a high paying job so that I could live in material comfort. However, when I didn't get accepted to Stanford and ended up attending Pepperdine instead, it started me down a path where I met an entirely different group of people and had an entirely different set of experiences. As I look back now I can see that the path through Pepperdine was what I really needed. It allowed me to have experiences that helped me to learn the skills I needed to find and pursue my true purpose in life. So I needed the "disappointment" of not getting in to my school of choice to be able to be on the path that led to my greatest benefit.

However, even though our pre-birth intentions play a powerful role in what happens in our lives, we still need to exercise our free will to find and follow our true purpose, and thus, experience our true joy. So in this regard we have to keep in mind that we will definitely NOT accomplish anything that we don't intend to do or don't believe that we can do. This is why we cannot be passive and we must actively work to find and live in accordance with our purpose. A big part of this task is to use the power of intention. When we visualize and intend in concert with our purpose in life, then we become powerful creators.

Everything in the Universe is energy and this includes our thoughts. So anytime we want to accomplish something, if we put out the strong thoughts and intention that it is going to happen, it is sending energy out from our minds into the world and is creating a path that will help us accomplish our goals. If we think that we are not able to accomplish something or that something cannot happen, then we are sending energy out into the world that is creating blocks and obstacles to those things happening.

A few years back Anni and I were becoming entrepreneurs and one of my jobs was to write the business plans. I hated doing this and constantly procrastinated. Every time I sat down to work on them I would find incredibly fascinating emails or news stories to distract myself from this task. When I wrote, I would labor over each sentence and even when I would make some progress it took me about ten times as much time and effort as it should have. Then one night what I had heard and read about intention finally clicked for me. So when I sat down to work, I took a few minutes and focused on exactly what I wanted. I wanted to write these certain sections, I was going to write these certain sections. When I put these intentions out into the universe, I did so with a specific strength of thought and purpose and I visualized the energy from these thoughts leaving my head and paving the way for me. This made an incredible difference. The tide of energy that I was usually fighting against, the one that made procrastination the path of least resistance was gone. I was able to write the sections in record time and with much less effort.

Another example of this principle in my life was when I was starting to write this book. I had the same problems as with the business plans: procrastination, falling asleep every time I sat down at the computer to write, etc. This time, the problem was that I didn't believe that I was good enough or enlightened enough to be a spiritual teacher or to bring forth a book that could help people change their lives. I had been getting a lot of spiritual inspiration and guidance that this is what I was supposed to do, but I was still thinking that some magical transformation would have to happen to me before I would be worthy of this work. Needless to say, while I was stuck in this belief system the work did not go anywhere and it produced a lot of frustration. Then, finally, after an especially illuminating dream that Anni had, it clicked for me. I was ready. I knew enough, I had experienced and accomplished enough and I was the right person for this job. Then, along with continuing efforts to see myself as this teacher, I began to believe that I was capable of this work and that it truly was my destiny. Once this shift occurred in my mind the book started to come through me and down onto paper. It started slowly but then gained momentum and the more that I focused on the fact that this was what I wanted to do and what I was meant to do the faster and easier it came.

What I have also learned from working with intention in this way are two things (1) shifting intention really is just a matter of changing our minds and (2) changing our minds isn't always all that easy. There is no secret trick to putting out an intention, but the key is that we have to be able to get to the point where our subconscious mind believes in what we are intending. For example, if our subconscious minds have been conditioned for a lifetime (or longer) that we are poor, that we deserve to be poor and that we always will be poor, then just saying that we want to be rich will not be enough. We need to do the work to change that belief in our subconscious minds to match the intention that we want to hold in our conscious minds.

There are a variety of tools and technologies available today to help us to align the beliefs that we hold in our subconscious with what we are intending in our conscious minds. These techniques range from repeating a simple mantra to self-hypnosis and Neuro-Linguistic Programming (NLP). I have tried them all and found that regardless of the method I use, the most important factor was to begin with the intention that I could align my subconscious and conscious minds with what I want. Regardless of what practice or method that we decide to use, the change is made only in our minds and deciding that we are able to make this change and that we ARE going to make this change clears the path to be able to get clear about the work in front of us. We just need to remember that everything is energy, our minds control the flow of energy and we need to recognize that we have this power and begin to use it consciously to move ourselves into the flow of our lives.

Take Action

> *If anything is worth doing, do it with all your heart.*
> -- The Buddha

Once we have decided to change our lives the next step is to take action. Action is such a critical step because it is translating our intentions into the material world and demonstrating to ourselves, others and all creation that we are serious and committed about making these changes.

For many years after I became interested in spirituality and how to create a better life for myself I immersed myself in books, recordings and even the occasional seminar focused on spiritual growth and self-improvement. My experience of life did improve some with what I was learning, but my obstacle was that I wasn't doing much with the knowledge. Each book just spurred the next book and while that has served to build a foundation for the work that I am doing today, I wasn't feeling the 'a ha!' of a life transformation. For all of the learning and knowledge, I didn't really change what I did all that much. It wasn't until I embraced a mantra of GOYA (get off your ass!) that my experiences started changing dramatically.

Very often we are in such a place of confusion and/or depression that we have no idea what we should do. If this describes where you are now, make your first action something aimed towards figuring out what you should do. For example, start a meditation practice or yoga class, seek out help from someone you trust. Remember that spirit is trying to help you so just get quiet and listen. Once you have intended to find and get yourself into the flow of your life, spirit will be screaming help to you at the top of its lungs! Obviously, this is a metaphor since, as far as I am aware, spirit does not have actual lungs. Therefore, the help will come to you in the form of new ideas, inspiration and coincidences. For example, if you decide that you want to change your life and then a friend recommends a book, or you have an opportunity to attend a seminar or a class, then take advantage of it. Similarly, in the same situation say you have a moment of inspiration and think, "I should go back to school," "I should find a new job," or whatever else comes along, then GOYA! Take a first step, get an application, put out your resume, network with new groups of people. Everyone's life path is different so you must learn to hear your own spiritual guidance. Your answers lie within you, so look there for how to best start the work. The only mistake that you can make on this path is to not begin!

A few years back I was going through my mail and I received a brochure from the Shambhala Mountain Center, a spiritual retreat center located high in the Rocky Mountains outside of Denver, CO. As I idly paged through it (probably because I was avoiding writing a business plan) a workshop on Energetic Healing and Shamanism offered by Alberto Villoldo jumped out at me. There was just something about it and I knew that I wanted to go to it. This was unusual as I was not particularly interested in energy healing, I didn't know anything about Shamanism, we had absolutely no money and given the fact that we have 3 young children, traveling out of town for a few days seemed an impossibility. Yet for some reason the idea of attending this workshop persisted.

I talked to Anni about it and she was supportive. The workshop was relatively low cost and I was able to get a frequent flyer airline ticket from Los Angeles to Denver so things started to fall into place. The kicker was that my daughter was offered a modeling job in Miami so Anni and our two youngest children were going to fly to Miami over that same weekend as the course and my sister was meeting them there to help. Talk about a coincidence! I knew that this could not have been random and that I should go.

However, as the workshop approached, the fear began to overtake me once more. I started to think that I shouldn't spend the money and just stay home. Then another "coincidence" occurred. I had started to read Villoldo's book, Shaman, Healer, Sage and one morning I was waiting in line to get through security at the Santa Monica Courthouse and there was a woman in front of me in line who kept turning around and looking back. Finally, she pointed to the book and said to me, "I know Alberto." I was amazed, apparently she was renting a house from him. I immediately knew that, again, this could not be just a coincidence and was spirit sending me another message to let go of my fear and go to the course. In the end, I did attend the weekend course and had some very intense energetic experiences that were critical for me to heal myself and take important steps toward being able to write this book.

While I am talking about learning to receive guidance from spirit, it is important that I share some more of my personal experiences in this regard. When I started this journey, I was so wounded, blocked off and full of fear that I could not hear spirit and often when I did receive inspiration I would be too afraid to act on it. So, beginning a few years ago, and greatly intensifying starting in December 2008, I have been contacted and given specific insight and instructions from spirit through my wife, Anni. Anni is very psychically open and has given Tarot Card readings and Spiritual counseling sessions for many years. She has been receiving guidance for me through readings, in her dreams and even during her meditations. In these instances spirit has taken different forms when speaking to her including different animals, an old shaman woman, my deceased Grandfather and even Jesus. It seems that spirit would take whatever form would have the most impact for me at the time and that communicated the message most effectively. Now I receive much of my guidance from spirit directly through inspiration, intuition and feeling.

Using an intermediary to hear spirit in the beginning was necessary for me because of my inability to hear the guidance myself. However, there are certain dangers of taking this route. For example, it is critical to find someone who is an effective reader and is sufficiently open to receive and interpret messages that you are unable to. As in any field there are psychics who are more competent than others. Even the competent ones are still human and can misinterpret information. For example, I once had a very powerful astrology reading and one of the things that the astrologer told me was that while I was born with very deep empathy and compassion for others, one of the big lessons that that I was here to learn was to be an individual, as well. I needed to learn how to not give away too much of myself. A few years later I went back to this interpretation to justify reducing the time and effort that I spent helping others to focus more on my own work. At that time, Anni received a message in a dream that the astrologer had misinterpreted the point (and/or I was misinterpreting her) and that my compassion was my greatest strength and that I should never throw it away or ignore it.

So even though I have received great help through psychic readings and highly recommend this if you feel stuck or you feel that you are not hearing spirit, I also urge caution in using and interpreting this information. Anni's advice to pass on in this regard is that any information that she receives for a client is something that they already know deep down. So if you receive advice through a psychic or spiritual reader that does not feel right and does not resonate with you at a deep level, then do not take it. Never believe anyone else's advice over what you feel is right.

In summary, remember that all of this is taking place in your mind and your exercise of free will are the choices that you make with regard to how you see, interpret and react to the circumstances of your life. However, while we are having physical experiences in this life, it is very important for us to take action in the physical realm consistent with our more enlightened thoughts. So GOYA and get out there because as you change yourself to live in peace and happiness, so you are changing the world!

Be Disciplined

More than those who hate you, more than all your enemies, an undisciplined mind does greater harm.
-- The Buddha

Discipline has been my biggest and hardest lesson to learn throughout this entire process. While many people seem to think that discipline is the ability to make yourself do something that you don't want to do, I view it as the ability to overcome fear, habit and other blocks to actually do what it is that you want to do. This is especially true when what you want to do is to make change in your life. The path of least resistance always seems to be the path that you are already on. The habits that we have developed over months, years and lifetimes have carved a deep rut that tends to keep us where we are. It can take a tremendous amount of energy to motivate you to jump out of that rut and to blaze a new path.

One would think that once I knew what I had to do to drastically change my life for the better, to become happier, healthier, richer, freer and in perfect harmony with my purpose in life that I would naturally just do it. Given the incredible benefits at stake, it seems as if the easiest choice in the world would be to just do what I know I need to do. However, my experience in this matter has been exactly the opposite. I was receiving extremely explicit, direct instructions from the divine for what I needed to be doing and yet, I was still procrastinating (at best) or just downright ignoring (at worst) these instructions. So my question to myself became, am I just an idiot or is there more to this?

People do what they feel will bring them the most happiness. Usually this determination of what will bring us the most happiness is made at a subconscious level, informed by deeply held beliefs and paradigms that are often at odds with what our intellectual mind knows to be true. For example, my intellectual mind knows that following a healthy diet with plenty of raw foods, exercising, expressing my creativity and working every free second of my life to pursue my purpose in life will bring the most spiritual clarity, fulfillment and happiness into my life in the shortest amount of time. However, over the years my subconscious has developed the habit of thinking that eating Reese's Cups and pizza, watching television and protecting myself by not venturing outside of my comfort zone is the best approach to life. In this situation, with no other outside forces, the subconscious was easily beating the intellectual portion of my mind.

However, there are times when outside forces are strong enough to tip this balance of power. For example, often when people have medical emergencies or near death experiences, such as a heart attack, they are able to drastically change their lifestyle. They lose weight, stop smoking and start exercising and experience a significant change in how they feel. However, many times after a short while, once the immediacy of the emergency has faded, they regress back to their old habitual programming.

So first, let's take a look at the cause of some of these deeply held self-limiting and self-destructive beliefs, using me as an example. Clearly my penchant for comforting myself with sweets and junk food is not an uncommon one and it stems from the fact that the high sugar and high carb foods that make me fat and sluggish also light up certain pleasure centers in my brain. This comforting effect is like a pain-killer on deeper feelings of loneliness and self doubt that I carry due to my belief in the separation that I talked about in Chapter 3. It is unfortunate and not uncommon that the coping mechanism that I have developed to deal with these feelings of separation are actually preventing me from attaining the wholeness that will replace all of those feelings with immense joy and peace.

A second issue that I have found with myself is that when I am faced with something new or different to do and it is not immediately clear to me how to do it or that I am able to do it or even if it seems like it will be unpleasant or annoying to do, then I will procrastinate to avoid testing myself. One example of this type of belief is that I have never viewed myself as a creative person. I never thought of myself as any good at art, painting or crafts. This became a real issue for me when I received instructions from my spiritual guide to perform a creative project. My task was to go and sit under a certain tree near the school where I work and meditate. Then after my meditation, I was supposed to look around and pick up whatever I saw on the ground and take it home and make three art projects and give them away as gifts. So I went and did the meditation, as instructed, and I picked up some leaves, twigs, a big stick, some fuzzy stuff and couple of Starburst wrappers and took it all home.

However, that is where the project stalled. I procrastinated, continually coming up with reasons why I should watch television rather than start on my project, or come up with some other art supply that I needed to buy before I could get started. Before I knew it several weeks had passed and by that time, I figured it was too late so I wrote off the project in my mind. That very night my spiritual guide came to Anni in a dream and really reamed me. It basically told me that I was screwing this whole thing up and I was wasting the incredible gift of this direct help and that if I ever didn't follow the guidance given to me again then it would stop coming and go help someone who would appreciate it. As was its intent, this message scared me enough to finally motivate me to sit down and do the projects. The amazing thing to me was that once I decided that I was going to do it, the project flowed. I was inspired to create and I made some pretty cool little sculptures out of the twigs and bark and then I wrote a poem to go along with the gifts.

So the moral of this story is that whether it comes from being yelled at by the spirits or the pain from your current way of living or the excitement of what is possible, what we call discipline is actually creating the desire, passion and energy to overcome and change your self-limiting and self-defeating subconscious programming and working to create new habits that support your growth and evolution rather than limit it. Really, what people call discipline is when you have good habits that support you rather than bad ones that keep you stuck.

Not everyone has issues with discipline. We all have our own personal strengths and weaknesses that come with us naturally. For example, Anni has less of a problem with motivating herself to start on a new project. Her natural makeup is that whenever she gets a new idea or is inspired to try something new, she spontaneously develops the passion that allows her to make the time and expend the effort to learn new things and create from her heart. If this sounds like you, then please focus on other areas that are holding you back. However, if you are more like me and tend to procrastinate and come up with a myriad of reasons why you can't change, why there isn't enough time, or the right conditions, etc. then here are a few tips that have helped me:

- **Eliminate the common distractions that feed your procrastination.**
For example, don't sit down and say, "I'm just going to watch this one show on TV and then start working on my stuff." Distractions like reading magazines, watching TV or even washing the dishes can easily consume an entire evening. GOYA and start your new habits now!

- **Hold yourself accountable.**
Tell as many people as possible about your goals and what you are trying to do and ask them to help to hold you accountable. The power of peer pressure doesn't end with middle school. Anything that you can do to raise the discomfort level for your failure to follow through on what you want can act as a catalyst for you to do it. For example, I attended a men's group where we would gather on the new moon, build a fire and listen to and support each other that was very helpful to me. Find a group like this or start one yourself.

- **Tell yourself that you are capable of doing what you want to do.**
Just the simple act of realizing that you don't believe in yourself or don't believe that you are capable of becoming who you want to become and then changing the inner story to telling yourself that you can is incredibly powerful. As I finally sat down and started typing into my computer to write this book I found that even though I had some ideas about what I wanted to say, everything that I wrote sounded horrible to me and I felt completely blocked. After a while, I received the guidance that I still wasn't believing that I could be a person to teach such profound lessons to people. Once I realized that this was my deep inner fear, I began focusing on telling myself that I was capable of being such a teacher. I began visualizing myself writing and teaching and being the person who I aspired to be. In a matter of days, this approach had completely changed the way I felt about writing and the words and ideas started to flow.

- **Do some energy work to remove deep-seated blocks**
Traumatic and emotional experiences that aren't processed or healed can

become trapped energy that is stored in our bodies. These trapped emotions can block the flow of energy in our bodies and result in subconscious blocks that make it difficult or impossible to move towards our bliss. These blocks can be processed and removed with different energy healing modalities such as Reiki, acupuncture, shamanic energy extractions to name a few. I will speak more to how I have removed trapped emotions in the next chapter.

The overall message on discipline is that if you are having trouble sticking to the work that you know you need to do and that you know you want to do, don't get down on yourself, but focus on nurturing your passion. Figure out what deep down limiting beliefs you carry that are getting in your way and chip away at them. Release the old patterns and replace them with your vision of what you want to be now. This focus will naturally generate the desire and passion to overcome whatever procrastination or other distractions that you face and allow you to get to work on creating your joyous life.

Be a Warrior for Happiness

Improvise, adapt and overcome
-- A mantra of the United States Marine Corps

Once you have developed your focus and are becoming disciplined in your work you are well on your way to being a warrior for your happiness. Believe me, you will need to be a warrior because once you decide that you want to walk this path and you want to learn how to leave your fears behind and live in joy there is no going back. To complete this transformation you will have to face your own deepest vulnerabilities and greatest fears. The only curriculum that will allow you to grow beyond these blocks and limitations is to practice through them. To do this will require you to be courageous and relentless in pursuit of your own healing and growth. As you face your own inner demons, at times it may seem easier to give up. Remember, if these issues weren't difficult, then they wouldn't be blocking you in the first place.

You will need to be relentless because your old life and old ways of thinking and doing things will constantly be trying to bring you back into the fold as you try to make a new life for yourself. Depending on how much progress your spirit self intended you to make in this lifetime, you may have provided yourself with many external experiences to remind yourself to wake up to the true reality and remember what it is that you really want.

Picture your life as a river and you come to a fork, a decision point. To the right is the direction of your spiritual growth, happiness, and smooth sailing in the flow of your life, and to the left are the choppy waters and turbulence of continuing to live out of habit and misunderstanding of life and your experiences. Sometimes, even after you have started down the right fork, you will row back upstream and into the left fork out of habit and conditioning where you will be thrown about by the raging waters. Often these difficulties will tend to pull you even deeper into the illusion of the material world. This is where you need to be relentless. The entire point of the difficult times is to remind you that you are on the wrong path and every time you are faced with them, you must, without fail, wake up, release what you are holding on to and start back down the correct path.

Looking back at myself, when I really began this journey in earnest, some of the major issues that I had to deal with were: (1) I had not found my voice and was not able to speak out for my beliefs (2) I had low self esteem and was afraid of being criticized (3) I was very concerned with making enough money to pay bills and be comfortable. So I'm sure that you will not be surprised that over the next few years after I decided that I wanted to travel the spiritual path I came face to face with all of these fears in big ways.

After leaving graduate school with my MBA, I went to work for a small company that was highly dependent on one client for its survival. After having a weird experience with this client myself, I became aware of several young interns and other employees who were having extremely bad experiences working at this client's offices. With the best of intentions I went to my company as a whistle blower, trying to protect our employees. Over the next year, I was in a situation where pressure continued to be applied to me to be quiet and stop advocating for what I felt to be right. I was incredibly uncomfortable with any type of conflict, let alone the lawsuits, personal attacks and loss of people who I thought were my friends that was to come. However, I was driven by the principles that I was standing up for and in the end, I found my voice, found my spine and learned to deal with criticism and attacks in a way that I had never imagined that I could.

Over the next few years I had: (1) cars repossessed on days that I was supposed to start a new job, (2) a business partner who constantly derided my integrity and competence and eventually abandoned the company causing it to fold, (3) extreme financial lack that led to more car repossessions, (4) personal bankruptcy and (5) eviction from my home, just to name a few of the highlights. As I dealt with these issues, they pushed me to the very edge. I had plenty of times when I didn't think that I could go on. I just wanted to give up. However, each time, I also found some way to keep coming back and to keep learning the lessons and then trying to apply them in these most intense circumstances. It was like the movie Rocky, even though I was getting my face rearranged by Apollo Creed, I just keep coming out for the next round. As I look back at these times, I can now see that each of these circumstances brought me face to face with my deepest fears and blocks. These blocks were limiting me, preventing me from reaching my potential and by working through them and gaining a deeper foundation, more self confidence and an ability and willingness to express my voice, I was growing into the person I needed to be in order to embark upon my life's work. It is obvious now that this was the perfect curriculum that I needed (even though it was in the school of hard knocks) for me to live a more free, joyful and fulfilling life.

Being a warrior means being disciplined, strong, relentless, ever-vigilant and to never give up. Change is difficult - very, very difficult. From my old high school physics class I remember Newton's second law of motion, which says (more or less) that you have to apply a force in order to get anything to change. This is what a warrior does, he or she brings strength of mind (and to some extent strength of body) to carry out his or her intentions. However, to be a warrior for happiness does not mean to battle, attack or destroy others, because these actions are what create unhappiness. Always remember that we are constantly trying to move from separation to wholeness. Resistance and attack, even if you are attacking a bad habit, annoying person or horrendous circumstance, still keeps you in separation and away from your joy. Instead, you want to befriend, understand and transform your adversaries. If something scares you, hurts you or just generally makes your life miserable, don't run away from it. Go into it, get to know it, figure out why it bothers you, then you can see through its illusion and take back the power that it has over you.

The purpose of life is to provide us with the fertilizer, the building blocks, for us to grow, blossom and evolve into beings who are fully engaged in life, full of love and compassion and bursting with joy. Therefore, take everything that happens, everything that you consider bad and compost it, transform it into healing energy. That is, confront your fears and heal them. As long as you remember that everything that happens to you in life was created by you for your own benefit, then nothing can harm you and you will come into your power as the divine being that you are.

Hooah great warriors! GOYA and go!

Integrate

> *It is called a path because you need to walk it.*
> *-- Native American Saying*

Some of the first guidance that I received from Spirit as I traveled down this road was that I had a lot of knowledge and concepts in my head, but that I had not integrated it into my body and being. Learning is useless unless you use it, live it and apply it on a daily basis. In my case especially, I had learned so much of the wisdom of the great teachers and traditions and yet, I was still keeping it all to myself and not fully demonstrating it or teaching it. It is the same for you as you do this work. This book and many others contain the information, concepts and paradigms that can help you to shed your limitations. However, much like learning how to swim, you can read books and watch instructional videos and be able to expound upon the fine points of every stroke, but in order to actually be able to swim, you need to get wet.

Like riding a bike, the work of moving from separation to wholeness is difficult at first. You are constantly thinking about everything, how am I pedaling, how am I balancing, how am I steering, and you will, without fail, fall down plenty of times. However, each fall is a valuable learning lesson in and of itself and after awhile, riding the bike becomes completely integrated into your body so that you never think about it, you just hop on and go.

During one of her conversations with my spirit guides, Anni asked how I was supposed to go about integrating all of my spiritual knowledge into my body. The answer was, "He just has to decide to do it." This is a reminder that all of this work actually takes place in our minds and then the results will show up in our bodies and in our actions and ultimately in our lives. However, don't get stuck in your thinking mind like I often have, practice it, live it, create and live from your body. Use it to help others. That's why you have one.

Purify

I cannot say this enough, we are all made up of pure energy. However, energy at different levels of vibrations has different qualities. As a result of this fact, we experience ourselves on four levels: (1) as a body, (2) as a mind and thoughts, (3) as an energy field and then, ultimately, (4) as pure spirit. The realm of the body is most familiar to all of us and is how most of us see ourselves most of the time. I am this body. I experience the world through its five senses. I feel its pains and pleasures and, ultimately, I am concerned with its safety, health and wellbeing. This view results in me seeing myself in competition with other bodies for the resources that I want and need. At the level of the mind, we usually experience ourselves as that "voice in our heads" whose job it is to analyze the information collected by the body and then tell us stories about what is happening to our bodies and how we should act and respond in the world. This mind shows up in our awareness as the voice that gives us a constant running commentary on everything and everyone. This is primarily the conscious mind. We are less aware of our unconscious mind or subconscious. However, this aspect of our minds is just as important as the conscious mind in that it holds the beliefs and templates that define the assumptions that the conscious mind uses to categorize the world.

This is where our view of ourselves generally stops, as a body with its own mind. However, we each also have our own subtle energy field associated with our body. This is energy that flows through and around our body and accounts for what people refer to as our auras. Most of us cannot see this energy field, but one aspect of shamanic training through the ages has been to be able to perceive these energies and to use that perception to help people to heal wounds (physical and emotional). This energy field is able to send and receive information, it acts a record of past wounds and hurts, especially emotional/psychological ones. However, we all perceive this energy field in ourselves and others, but just not in a way that we understand or value very highly. For example, when you meet someone who "lights up a room" or someone who can "bring a room down in an instant" then we are perceiving certain aspects of their energy field. Similarly, intuition and "gut feelings" are also us receiving information through our energy field rather than through the traditional five senses.

Ultimately all separation comes from being wounded, so the path back to wholeness requires healing. This subtle energy field is the basis for many healing systems such as shamanism, acupuncture, Reiki and the Rising Star Healing System. The reason that these healing approaches focus on our personal energy field is that this field carries the blueprint for our bodies and greatly affects our thinking minds. Therefore, all disease, while it manifests on the level of the body or, in the case of psychosis, the thinking mind, has its root in our subtle energy field. So if we treat a disease on the level of the body, we may be able to eliminate symptoms, which can be very useful, but unless we change the blueprint at the level of our energy field we are bound to experience that problem, or something similar, again.

The same goes for our thought patterns and feelings of disconnect, loneliness, sadness and depression. While some of these may seem to be caused by chemical imbalances in our brains or negative thought patterns, the reason that this ultimately occurs is that our energy field contains blocks, wounds or other aspects that tend to foster and support such thought patterns. So as with physical disease, when we attempt to make a change in our condition, it would seem to make sense to work at the level of the our energy field as well as that of the body and mind, because, if you don't clear the imprint of a certain condition, then no amount of work on your body or mind will ever fully heal you. And remember, in the work of this book our entire goal is to achieve the healing necessary to move us away from separation to a place of wholeness which will bring us peace, happiness and joy.

The final level of how we can, and will, experience ourselves is as pure whole spirit. This is the experience of oneness with all and everything. Uninterrupted and eternal, this state of being is the ultimate destination for us all, often called enlightenment or returning to God.

There are two main reasons that we want to raise our energy level and clear any blocks that may be stuck in our energy field: (1) to clear the negative imprints in our energy fields that are keeping us locked into our current patterns of suffering and unhappiness and (2) to tune in to help from our spirit guides.

As I discussed at length above, the hurt and wounds that you carry in your energy from past experiences can profoundly affect your current experience of life. Most of my life, until recently, I have been prone to negative thoughts and depression and I have had trouble expressing myself to others, especially in situations where I am not sure if they will like what I am saying or if my words are likely to cause conflict. These habitual ways of thinking and acting have been major blocks to my personal growth, spiritual growth, and the writing of this book, especially.

Several weeks before my trip to Colorado to attend Alberto Villodo's seminar, I received some guidance from my spirit guides, through Anni, that told me that I had suffered a great wounding in a previous life (2 lifetimes ago to be precise) and that I still carried this wound and the associated anger with me. Furthermore, this anger was dominating my life and preventing me from moving forward and seizing my destiny. This made me even more excited about attending the seminar as shamanism is all about healing these types of wounds so I was thinking that something was going to happen to me at the seminar to help to heal this wound and allow me to move forward.

On the third and last day of the seminar I was getting a little concerned because I had not felt like I had even found out what my main problem was, let alone heal it. Then we started doing an exercise called soul retrieval. The idea behind this concept is that under conditions of extreme pain and suffering it is possible for a part of our soul to separate from the rest of us and become dormant in order to escape intense pain. This further separation of our spirit from itself and others leads to even more unhappiness and sadness in our lives.

We did this exercise with a partner, where we would each do a guided meditation to seek out any separated pieces of our partner's soul and bring the lost piece back to our partner along with any messages or learnings from the separation. When my partner shared with me her experience in her guided meditation, it knocked me over. When she journeyed down into the spirit world in her meditation she found a little infant baby on the ground (me). She picked me up and was transported to a beach. Where she was told the following story:

Two lifetimes ago, I was born to two parents, a mother who wanted me and a father who did not . The father abused me severely when I was a baby and I died as an infant from that abuse.

This story triggered a rush of insight and understanding on my part. The pain from these events and my inability, at the time, to defend myself in any way caused a portion of my soul to shut down and also imprinted my energy field so that in my current lifetime I tried to create a cocoon of protection around myself that prevented me from living and experiencing joy and happiness in an effort to try to minimize the chance of getting hurt again. I tried to eliminate even the smallest opportunity for criticism so I took no risks, tried nothing new and did not let anybody or anything penetrate this protective layer.

In her vision, my partner saw, as a symbol of the gift available to me in this lifetime, a huge beautiful mountain with a golden temple at the top. She took the baby back to the beach and held the baby tight and loved it at which point the baby started to smile and kick its legs, happy. Then she looked into the ocean and saw a huge great white shark that was there to protect me. Then she brought back the message of protection and the lost piece of my soul and she symbolically offered it back to me. As I accepted it, I felt an intense tingling sensation throughout my body, especially up and down my spine. I felt whole again.

While this was the penultimate experience of a very intense weekend for me and it sparked a great deal of healing, as I returned home I still felt that I carried with me negative energy imprints that were blocking me from freely expressing myself. For several years prior to the weekend retreat, whenever I would go running and really get my energy flowing I would begin to gag and have dry heaves. While I rarely actually vomited, it felt as if energy was coming up from my stomach, through my throat and out of my mouth. In addition, I had recently learned an exercise from Villoldo's book that aimed to clear negative energy from your chakras (seven main energy centers located along your spine). In this exercise, whenever I would activate my throat chakra I would get the same gagging and dry heaving as when I would run. This phenomena persisted even after my soul retrieval experience, so I came to the conclusion that I still carried negative energy with me.

I did an online search and found my local neighborhood shaman, Joye Peters. Of course, a year earlier I wouldn't have imagined that there were shamans around Los Angeles, but as you progress down your spiritual path, it is amazing the new doors and worlds that open up to you. Anyway, she performed energy extractions on me in two sessions. An energy extraction is where a shaman is able to release negative imprints from your energy field. During the first session I didn't feel anything, but at the end Joye looked like hell. Even though I didn't see, hear or feel anything during the extraction, the next day I felt like an entirely new person. My being felt incredibly free and I had a lightness about me that I could not remember ever experiencing before. I knew that nothing could bother me, even in situations that would usually stress me out. I was just smiling and happy. It was amazing.

The night after the initial energy extraction I had a very interesting dream. In the dream I was fighting with 3 criminals. I easily vanquished the first two, but the third was a huge guy who resembled the wrestler Andre the Giant. I went after Andre with a pipe and he just grabbed it out of my hand and laughed at me. So after waking up I figured that there was still a fairly strong dark energy hanging around me and I scheduled a second session for a few weeks later.

Within a week after the first session I had integrated the changes that happened to me and I became used to my new feelings of lightness and joy. When the second session came around Joye came back to my house and was doing her thing and this time Anni was with us meditating during the extraction process. At the end of the extraction process both Anni and Joye received a bolt of communication from Spirit at the same time saying to focus the extraction on my throat area. As Joye did it, she perceived removing a negative imprint in the form of a snake that went from my throat all the way down to my left big toe. Again, I didn't feel a thing. However, afterwards Anni told me that during her meditation she had a vision. The vision was that I was walking next to Jesus (yes THE Jesus). Anyway, at the time when Joye removed the big snake, in Anni's vision I collapsed into Jesus' arms. As he held me he touched my forehead and planted the seed of a new soul. This was representing my opportunity to start over again without the baggage that I had lived with for my entire life. Again, the next day I felt once again completely invincible and at a level of lightness and joy that I had not known existed. These experiences didn't magically make me a fully enlightened person, but they removed some of the blocks that were making it more difficult for me to practice happy and find and live my purpose in life. It is as if I was born with heavy metal chains wrapped around my feet and I was trying to train for a marathon. Removing the chains won't automatically make me a great runner or do the training for me, but it will sure make it easier for me to do the work necessary to reach that goal.

Now, as I reflect on a story like this about my experience I realize that some readers will have some familiarity or experience with this type of energy work and some readers will be completely bewildered and very skeptical (to say the least). If you fall into the second category, please realize that this is where I would have been reading this several years ago. However, the reason that I share this is that I now know that this type of energy work is effective and it can be a great aid to anyone who is attempting to grow and evolve into a happier person. The Buddha once told his followers not to believe anything that anyone said, not even him. However, they should try out what they hear and only accept what they find to be useful. So I encourage all of you to try some type of energy work, put out the intention to find the best fit practitioner for you and withhold judgment until you have seen whether this offers immediate and significant benefits to you or not. Based on my personal experience, I feel that you will find an incredible potential for growth and healing. I know I have.

Subsequent to my experiences with energy extraction I came across another method for removing the energetic blocks that hold us back and can eventually cause disease. This method is very simple and, with some training, you can learn to do it yourself or find one of the growing number of practitioners who offer it. It is called The Emotion Code and has been developed by Dr. Bradley Nelson. This method uses muscle strength testing to communicate directly with your subconscious mind. By asking your subconscious yes and no questions you are able to identify trapped emotions and then release them using a magnet. I watched a webinar on Dr. Nelson's website and listened to his E-book and was practicing this on myself and family within a week. I have gotten amazing results, similar to those that I experienced with the energy extractions. I highly recommend checking out this healing modality to clear emotional blocks as well.

The other key reason to purify is that by physically and mentally purifying yourself from low vibration energy blocks, you make yourself into a better receiver for the help and messages that are coming to you from your inner spiritual guides. Earlier, I used the analogy of a radio receiver that needs to tune to a specific frequency in order to receive a radio broadcast. This is the same with us. We have a constant source of help and information available to us from our spirit guides. However, in order for us to access it, we need to raise our own personal vibrations to match that of the help coming to us. There are three main reasons that we do not "hear" and understand these messages: (1) our bodies and minds are bogged down with low vibrational energies and toxins that make us poor receivers for this information, (2) our minds are so cluttered with constant thoughts, worry and anxiety that the guidance that we need gets drowned out, and (3) even when we do receive inspired ideas we don't trust ourselves enough to recognize them for what they really are and we write them off as crazy or pie in the sky dreams.

A first step to purifying and raising our personal vibrational levels is something that we all know that we should do anyway. That is, improve our diets and exercise more. Toxins have low vibrational energies, so the more of these substances that we put into our bodies the lower our body energy will vibrate. Eating only organic foods and raw vegan diets will greatly support the rise of your vibrational level. This is why many people have experienced miracle cures of physical maladies after switching to raw super-healthy diets. I even have a friend who went to a completely raw diet and she has reported amazing increases in her intuition and psychic abilities since making the change. Because of this, I can't recommend anything less than this ideal. However, I also want to stress that this is not an all or nothing endeavor and there is no specific body weight or shape that you are shooting for. Any incremental improvements that you make in how you treat your body will make incremental improvements in your vibrational level and, thus, how you feel and how you are able to take control of your life and practice happy. From a personal front I still have many bad habits in this arena that I developed over a lifetime and I still eat some fast foods, processed foods and sugary drinks. However, as I have changed these habits and improved by diet, my general energy as well as my overall outlook on life and ability to practice happy has greatly improved and my enjoyment of life improved along with it.

As we evolve our physical bodies in this way, I also recommend integrating more physical movement and exercise into your life that are specifically designed to help raise your vibrational energies and open you up to spiritual guidance and communion. Whether you get into yoga, tai chi or some form of sacred dance, these practices can greatly advance you on the way accessing your inner guidance and living the life that you are meant to live.

In addition to changes on the physical level, some form of meditation is critical to this path. Many people think of meditation as sitting on a pillow with your legs crossed chanting "om". This has been a very effective approach for many people, but really, what you are trying to accomplish with meditation is to give your mind the space to quiet and let go of the usual frenetic internal monologue that you have come to consider as normal. This can be done through a variety of practices. For example many people attain this state through writing, painting, long distance running, hiking in the woods, knitting, crochet, etc. Just about anything that gives you something to concentrate on that will occupy your conscious mind and allow the silence, beauty and inspiration that come with it, rise to the forefront.

Once you go to the effort of being in silence and opening yourself to communication and guidance from your inner self, you need to listen to it. If you put an intention out that you want to know your purpose in life, then when you start getting ideas or dreams about doing something different, DON'T IGNORE THEM. The more unhappy, anxious and depressed that you feel, the more likely it is that your calling in life is quite different from what you are currently doing. Therefore, if you are currently working as an accountant and you start getting ideas that you want to teach math to children, stop telling yourself that it is impossible, that it is too late, that you can't make enough money as a teacher, etc, etc. GOYA! It is NOT just an idle daydream. If you are getting these ideas, then act on them – at least try them out. That doesn't necessarily mean that you need to quit your job today and go knocking on the doors of local schools looking for a teaching job (though sometimes that may be what it means). Take some purposeful action. Find out what the requirements are to become a teacher. Take some courses, volunteer as a tutor for underprivileged children. Just take the first small steps towards fulfilling that dream. If you do this with the trust that you will be shown the way, then, if it is the right path, the next door will open up, the next opportunity will present itself and so on. This is how we find our way into the flow of our lives. However, to do this, we must make ourselves better receivers so that we can hear and use the guidance that is available for us.

Practice, Practice, Practice

Happiness is a skill to be learned and practiced. It is actually unlearning all of the false and incorrect habits and ways of thinking that we now hold, but either way, we need to work at it. To become happier we need to go into training, like an athlete, a dancer or a musician. We need to establish our workouts and then stick to them, practicing regularly and through repetition and increasing the intensity of the workouts/practices, then we improve our skills.

We cannot become prima ballerinas unless we master the most difficult steps and positions, and the old adage that we must learn to walk before we can run is very true. At first, we struggle to learn the basics and fail often – nobody ever succeeds at difficult things on the first try. Even though we fall down, with persistence, we increase our skill, improve our technique and build stamina to the point where we are able to pull off basic moves with focus and thought. As we continue to improve, the basic skills become automatic and we move onto more and more difficult feats. Finally, when we become masters, the skills that we have learned are completely integrated into our bodies and beings so that they are like breathing. We embody it.

As we continue to practice our Happiness Workout, we will see the results all along the way. At first we will notice things that used to bother us we now let go. Times when we would go into a funk or depression, we are able to stay on an even keel. Even when we do fall into our old patterns, we now notice them and are able to pull ourselves back out instead of languishing in dread. The better we get at it, the happier we are and the lighter our life becomes. Soon, even Thanksgiving dinner with the in laws becomes an occasion where you can't stop smiling and you just enjoy the bliss of life while appreciating the beauty in everything and everyone all the while letting the stress of everyone around you just pass right through without effect. I know this last one may sound a bit far fetched, but it is there for us all.

As an example, for the last few years my family's financial situation has been a total wreck. Since I was fired from my job for being a whistle blower we have not had a steady source of income and have lived in a constant state not knowing where the money was going to come from to support even the most basic of necessities, including housing, food, gas for the car, etc. In the beginning, this left me in a constant state of stress and anxiety. I constantly ran through scenarios in my mind of how we were not going to have enough money to pay for this, we were going to become homeless, we weren't going to have enough food for the kids to eat, etc. As you can imagine, with my view of life mainly focusing on the physical world and not having integrated a higher broader view of what was happening into my thinking I was depressed and full of despair. Moreover, every time it seemed like we saw what seemed like an opportunity to get out of the situation, a potential job, an investor for our company, etc. it would evaporate and not come to fruition. In some ways, this was even more frustrating and would feel like a kick in the gut from the Universe that made me question why I was even alive.

Luckily, I was able to consciously use these painful experiences to keep me motivated to practice the techniques that I outline in this book and, over time, I was able to become more and more able to view these situations in a larger context and increase my level of trust in the wisdom of what was happening. One typical example is the time that we were waiting for an offer on one of Anni's books that was promised by a publisher several weeks before. We were very anxious for this because the advance from this book could sustain us for several months, buy Christmas presents for the kids, catch up on rent payments, etc. Well, we got word that they changed their minds and were not going to make the offer. It was a tough one to take because we had allowed ourselves to become attached to it happening and were counting on it. However, even though it was definitely a let down for me, the reaction of trusting that this is the right path, that everything is going to work out and to look for the gift and learning in it for me allowed me to come through it with barely a blip on my emotional radar, whereas two years earlier I would have been literally crying myself to sleep at night sure that this was going to mean disaster for our life. So, while what I am proposing won't guarantee an easy, annoyance-free life, what I do promise is that if you break your old destructive habits around how you view the world and the meaning that you give to your life circumstances, you will live a happier, more peaceful and fulfilling existence, no matter what happens around you. You will take your power back from your ego and you will have control of how you experience your life.

CHAPTER 6

THE HAPPINESS WORKOUT

Overview of the workout

Any time you go into training, it is good to have a plan and structure to make sure that you are covering all of the bases. So here I am providing a very condensed overview of what I am calling The Happiness Workout and then I will go into more detail on each suggestion in the following pages.

Create strong positive intentions to create a clear picture of what you want:

1. Start the day by stating your intention for how you want your day to go.
2. Work with a mantra. Have it written down, carry it with you and come back to it whenever you remember or have a free moment during the day, like while driving or waiting in line.
3. Create a vision board and keep it visible and updated.

Clear your energy:

4. Spend 30 minutes in the morning exercising. This can be walking, running, yoga, tai chi, surfing etc. Something that stretches and animates your body and gets your energy flowing.
5. Eat healthy foods, the more raw food such as fruits and vegetables the better and cut back on sugary processed stuff.
6. As needed see an energy healer/practitioner such as an acupuncturist, shaman, reiki master, etc. Use the tools and techniques of these practitioners to identify and clear energetic blocks that can affect not only your physical health but also your spiritual growth. You can also learn and use self-help techniques

for this purpose such as the Emotion Code, Theta Healing® or similar program.

7. Invite joy into your life.

Listen to the guidance that is available for you:

8. Spend 30 minutes in the morning in meditation. Invite your spirit guides and/or higher self into your consciousness and ask for guidance to be given to you throughout the day.

9. If needed visit an energy reader or psychic counselor. These people can help you to identify blocks and access the guidance offered to you by spirit guides when you are not able access them by yourself. Again, please be aware that these people are humans and the information that you gain from them is being filtered and interpreted by their egos, so please test everything that you hear with your own heart and only accept those things that resonate strongly with you. A great reading will be one in which after a few days you will be able to say to yourself that deep down you already knew this, but had not been able to face it yet.

Live in your flow:

10. Be generous. Give a gift to someone who didn't ask for it and do not ask for anything in return. If they offer repayment, ask them to pay it forward to someone else who needs it instead. Give to others throughout the day. Pay the bill for the person behind you in the drive-thru, stop and offer help if you see someone struggling with many packages or has a flat tire. Give freely of your time, money and attention when people don't expect it and see the difference it makes in your own life.

11. In everything, give thanks. Find the beauty in everything that happens in your life. Treat every wonderful aspect of your life and every difficulty as sacred gifts worthy of your gratitude. Remember, this is help given to you by yourself so make sure that you receive the gift and use it to your best advantage.

12. Stop reliving negative experiences over and over again.

13. Do things that are difficult for you or that you are afraid of or that you think you cannot do. I call these exercises "Fear-Outs".

14. Forgive relentlessly and completely.

Create your intentions

The first book that I read when I began my path to self discovery and spiritual growth was Stephen Covey's *Seven Habits of Highly Effective People*. One of Covey's habits that really stuck with me was, "Begin with the End in Mind". The simple idea of deciding where you want to go is a huge leap forward in moving from being at effect in your life (where the circumstances and situations that you experience control you) to being at cause (where you take responsibility for and control of your own happiness).

Visualizing what you want is a widely taught technique for self improvement and creating what you want in life (manifestation). However, simply visualizing what you want is not enough. It is critical that you actually make a strong decision that this is what you are going to be, this is how you are going to live, this is what you will achieve. By deciding you leave behind all doubt and equivocation and you have created the desired situation in your mind. Now it is possible for a path to get from where you are to where you want to go to appear. This knowledge of where you want to be also makes it easier to make decisions about prioritization. Do the things that take you towards your goal and lower the priority or don't do the things that don't take you in that direction.

Remember, if you put out an intention to do something, you MUST make sure that you believe that your desire is possible. One of the biggest blocks to me writing this book was my belief that I wasn't capable of doing it. I didn't think that I was spiritual enough to write and teach this type of material. I just didn't think that I had it in me. In actuality, it was a manifestation of low self-esteem that I wasn't good or capable enough to fulfill this destiny. However, once I became aware of this block and brought it out from the unconscious to the conscious mind I was able to dispel it. These types of limiting beliefs are only powerful when they live in the unconscious without you being aware of them. In the subconscious they are able to control your thoughts and actions without you knowing it. Once you are able to see these limiting beliefs, you can make the simple decision to change them and your life takes a sudden turn in the direction of your desires.

Back in 1999 just before my first marriage ended, my ex and I went to marriage counseling. She dropped out, but I still went to see the therapist for a few more visits. In one of these visits, the therapist asked me why I assumed that everyone I met didn't like me even though there was clear evidence to the contrary. It was like a light bulb went on in my head. Yes, of course that's what I was doing, but I didn't realize it. Right then and there I decided that this low self-esteem was not serving me and was a ridiculous way to live my life and I decided to change this. However, especially in the beginning, whenever I would be in an uncomfortable or new situation those same feelings would arise in me, but now I had the power of knowledge, which gave me the ability to choose my reaction differently. I would tell myself that my assumption that this person does not like me is not true and I would choose to react as if it were not true. In addition, exercises such as forcing myself to smile and say hello as I passed by people have made an enormous difference in replacing my old limiting belief with a new productive one. Now, even though I still feel the echoes of the old habits, I am much more at ease and comfortable in situations that used to make me tense and anxious.

Once you have decided what changes you will make in your life, then everything that happens is there to help you on your way to achieving these goals. Sometimes it will be in the form of coincidences or opportunities to move in that direction and sometimes it will be challenges designed to help you to learn the lessons and develop the skills and capabilities that you will need to fulfill your destiny. However, no matter what the form, it is your job to see the beauty and the gift in every situation and to use it to your full advantage. I talk more about this in the section on living in your flow.

Exercise: Decide to do it!

Every morning when you first wake up and before you get out of bed, set clear intentions for the day. How you want to be, how you want to feel, what you want to accomplish, etc. Spend whatever time you can and that feels right, but I would suggest aiming for 5 minutes of focused intention time before hitting the shower.

Exercise: Write a mantra and use it!

A mantra is a few line poem or saying that is meant to program your subconscious mind to be in alignment with what you have decided. It is designed as a way to alter the most ingrained underlying limiting beliefs. I like ones that rhyme because I have an easier time remembering them and saying them. You should repeat your mantra, with focus and intention, as often as possible, while driving, waiting in line, exercising, on hold, etc. Here are some examples of mantras consistent with the approach outlined in this work that you can use in addition to or instead of one that you develop that is more specific to you.

I focus my energy to meet my destiny
living in my flow happy as can be

I act in love and integrity
and live in trust without fear and worry

I receive each gift with openness and gratitude.

Exercise: Create a vision board!

In addition to mantras, a vision board is a great way to focus on your goals and keep them in your consciousness. To create a vision board you will need a large piece of poster board or a cork bulletin board. Go through magazines, newspapers and your favorite websites and cut out pictures that represent to you where you want to go and what you want to accomplish. Create a collage on your board with these pictures and then hang the board in a place where you will see it every day. Take a few moments each day to look at the board and refocus yourself on what you want. Pinterest is also a great way to create a vision board in an electronic medium, but you need to make sure that you visit it as often as possible to keep the images bombarding your subconscious. The visual aspect of vision boards make them very effective tools or manifesting your desires.

Raise your energy

We are all pure energy. Modern physics says so, spiritual traditions say so and our day to day life experiences say so. Everything in the physical universe that we perceive, including ourselves, are bundles of vibrating, pulsing energy. Each entity in the universe has its own unique quality and vibration of energy. As human beings, we are born to seek growth and evolution to raise our energy vibrational levels ever higher. These higher vibrational levels bring us greater joy and happiness, greater love and enable us to understand and live out our purpose in life. You can raise your level of consciousness and thus, your vibrational level through the mind and how you choose to view, interpret and react to life. However, we can also affect our energy levels with actions taken on the physical level to complement and advance these practices.

Our minds are the source of everything that we experience in our lives, including our bodies. Everything from how we look to how we feel to the energy vibration levels have their source in our minds. This "mind-body connection" has communication in both directions. That is, by changing assumptions and thought processes in our minds we can change our bodies and by making changes on the physical level, we can have effects on our state of mind. This two-way communication between the body and mind is a foundational principle of many yoga practices and healing modalities.

Our goal here is to keep the energy flowing throughout our bodies to nurture our spiritual and physical selves as well as to raise the vibration of our energy field so that we can tune in to the help and guidance from our higher selves.

You are what you eat from your head right down to your feet
--A jingle that I remember from childhood.

This statement is obviously true in our lives. When Anni and I were operating our baby food company we often pointed out to potential customers that their babies will double in weight between ages 6 months and one year, and the food that they eat is what provides the material for this rapid body growth. We are in a similar situation, our entire physical bodies, blood, bone, skin and flesh are made of the foods that we eat. So to raise our energy levels we want to eat foods that are high in life energy and drink plenty of water to help to wash out the toxins that are already in your body. The more life that is in the food, the more life that it will impart to you as it incorporates into your body. You can tell what the right foods are for you because you feel good after eating them. This may be hard to tell at first as many of us are so bogged down with years of eating high sugar, highly processed foods that are full of chemicals (including pesticides). So I urge you to add more organic fruits and vegetables into your diet and as much raw food as possible. A good rule to consider is that foods that have a short shelf life and go bad quickly have "life energy" still. The ones with long shelf lives have already had the life taken out of them and are lifeless. The closer to the plant or vine that these foods are, the more "life energy" they have and when you eat them, this "life energy" is then incorporated into your body, helping to purify it and raise its energy level.

Similarly, physical exercise is a great way to increase the flow of energy through your body. In eastern thought the flow of energy through your body, qi (pronounced "chee"), is what gives your body life. Rigorous aerobic exercise, such as running, heats and strengthens this life force. Additionally, other stretching and movement practices such as yoga and Qigong are designed to remove blocks and open the channels for energy, allowing it to flow more freely throughout all parts of your body.

The mantra of "eat right and exercise" is nothing new, but is often not practiced fully. However, the benefits of these practices are critically important to raising the energy vibration and flow in our physical bodies to allow us to connect with our intuition and spiritual guidance. This connection is absolutely necessary to achieve greater clarity and direction in our lives and ultimately, to live more in joy and less in anxiety. This is not to say that sedentary people who eat nothing but fast food cannot possibly be happy or spiritually connected. If Jesus or Buddha decided to eat lunch at FatBurger on a regular basis I don't think it would have knocked him off his game, but if you are not where you want to be in your life right now, eating better and exercising more are practices that will help you move in the right direction.

There are many books, DVDs, studios and other outlets promoting different dietary approaches and exercise regimens, so I don't specify one here. Every person is different, so it is up to you find the diet and exercise program that works best for you. As with all things, focus on the intention to find the right approaches that will work for you and make an effort to seek them out and then you will receive the help. You will "randomly" come across a friend who loves their yoga studio or a new grocery store or dietary approach will pop into your awareness. Pay attention and then, when you see these signs, GOYA and take action, try them out, see how you feel. You will be able to see and feel the difference in your life.

Exercise: Meditate on raising your energy

Sit upright in a comfortable position. Close your eyes and bring your attention to your breath. Once you feel relaxed and comfortable, visualize a bright white light whose source is at the base of your spine in the center of your body. As you breathe out visualize the light rising up your spine, filling your body with white light. As you breathe in, visualize the light getting stronger and brighter. Then on the out breath again, see the light rising farther up your spine, filling you with white light. When the light reaches the top of your head, visualize it bursting through your head and shining up into the heaven, connecting you with your source. Do this practice every day to revitalize and cleanse your energetic body, raising your level of vibration.

Exercise: Infuse your body with the energy of your choice

Sit in a comfortable position and bring your focus to the here and now with a few deep, cleansing breaths. Visualize a ball of bright beautiful light, like a little sun, located about 18 inches directly above the top of your head. (this point is also known as the 8th chakra - where your physical being connects with your higher self). Next, ask your higher self for the gift of the frequencies of light that will bring you _____ (fill in the blank with what you are asking for such as physical or emotional healing, forgiveness, energy, courage, creativity, enlightenment, etc). Now, move your focus to your heart (4th chakra) and hold a deep sense and feeling of gratitude while the energy is downloaded into your heart. Anywhere from 15-30 seconds or more – just go until you feel that the process is finished. When you are ready, take several deep breaths and on each out-breath focus on moving the energy from your heart to every part of your body, feeding each cell with the light containing your gift. Make sure that you hold the strong intention of integrating the new energies into your body. (Note: an alternate method would be to hold a bottle of water in the palms of your hands and move the energy from your heart into the water, then as you drink the water, you are integrating the new energies into your body.

While these approaches can help you to clear and strengthen your personal energy field, sometimes you have wounds that are so deep or have been there so long that you need help to clear them. In these cases you need to seek the help of an energy practitioner who can address the issue from an energetic point of view and help to clear, heal and strengthen your energy field. Whether it be a shamanic healer, an acupuncturist, a reiki master or other healer the key is that the person is trained and experienced in identifying and clearing energy blocks or wounds. Once negative blocks are removed, it is critical for the practitioner to then strengthen and illuminate you, filling the void where the negative energy was with love and peace that will allow you to take the next steps in your growth.

Often these problems with our energy fields will end up manifesting themselves physically in the form of pain or disease, which can give us clues that we have these energetic blockages and where they are. However, sometimes the blockages manifest in more subtle ways such as minor physical limitations, depression, negative attitudes, low self-esteem, etc. But, a good energy worker will be able to diagnose and find these blockages without obvious physical ailments and help to give you a fresh start.

I started running in high school and pursued it on and off since then as a part of my physical fitness routine. Around 2002 or 2003 I started to develop the situation where whenever I would go for a run, at some point I would feel sick to my stomach and either vomit or have dry heaves. It wasn't very frequent at first, but by 2004 it was very noticeable to me and by 2008 it was severe and associated with not just running but any rigorous physical activity, including during breathing exercises while practicing Kundalini yoga.

In the Spring of 2009 I had signed up to go to a weekend workshop on Shamanic Healing with Alberto Villoldo. In advance of the workshop, I read his book Shaman, Healer, Sage. This book talks a lot about our personal energy field, how we carry the wounds from our past in this energy field, and how this record affects our physical bodies and health. One of the shamanic exercises that was recommended in this book was referred to as "Chakra Balancing". Chakra refers to one of 7 main energy centers in our bodies that run along our spine from the base of the spine to the top of the head (coccyx, sacrum, navel, heart, throat, forehead and top of head). Each chakra is a whirling vortex of energy that plays a key role in some aspect of our physical, emotional, mental and spiritual well-being. In the shamanic view, our chakras can get "clogged" by low vibration negative energies that act like a sludge and slow down the spinning of the chakra and thus, the flow of energy. The exercise, which was to be done in the shower, was to take your fingers directly in front of your body at each chakra point and spin them in a circle counter clockwise (as if you were facing yourself). This action is supposed to aid in back washing the energetic sludge. Then take your fingers as if scooping the sludge out of the chakra and wash it down the drain in the shower. When complete you would then spin your fingers in the opposite direction to speed the chakra up to its natural higher vibrational state. This should be repeated for each of the seven chakras.

This seemed like an easy enough exercise to try, so I started doing it in the shower one morning and when started working on my throat chakra the gagging and dry heaving started with a great intensity. As I was "scooping" the sludge out of this chakra I could feel energy coming from my stomach up my throat and out my mouth as I dry heaved. It was clear that it was an "energy" process that was also being mirrored by my physical reaction. Each time that I performed this exercise I had the exact same reaction with very intense dry heaves or vomiting whenever I interacted with my throat chakra in this manner.

One interesting insight that I gained from this practice is that the throat chakra is the one that is said to control self-expression and communication. This was especially interesting to me as my entire life I had always had trouble expressing myself, whether it be to avoid conflict, or because I was afraid of derision or that nobody wanted to hear what I had to say. So the fact that this energetic blockage was expressing itself so strongly as I was working to try to write this book and to become a teacher of these principles showed me that my issues around self esteem and communication had to be conquered before I could move forward to fulfill my destiny in this lifetime. However, to deal with something so apparently deep and rooted within me, I felt that I needed some help.

After attending my weekend workshop on shamanism, I was more convinced than ever that I needed to find a practicing shamanic healer to have this energy extracted from my throat chakra. I found a shaman in my area and had the energy extractions done (I described this experience in detail in Chapter 2). It was painless and I didn't actually feel anything while it happened, but afterwards I felt like an entirely new man. All of my problems and fears seemed easily manageable and not all that important anyway. My need for the people in my life to act a certain way had disappeared. I felt deep love for everything and everyone. This is not to say that I suddenly became enlightened, because over the course of a week or two this feeling integrated itself and some of my old bad habit thought patterns reappeared. However, it was like a process of taking 50 steps forward and 2 steps back. Now, when I do my chakra balancing exercise, I do not have the physical reaction, I have been able to make progress in expressing myself through writing and in all aspects of my life and I am continuing to progress down the road of my purpose in life.

I tell this story to reinforce the idea that I know, from first hand personal experience, that energies live within us and affect us physically, emotionally and psychologically. I urge everyone to find a great energy practitioner and work to address, at the energetic level, the wounds from our past that make us sick and continue to hold us back. However, as you interview a potential energy practitioner, please make sure that he or she is on the same wavelength and will be working to help you to find the major blocks that are holding you back. If an acupuncturist is just looking to help your arthritis or sore knee and not willing or capable to look for and treat the bigger blocks that affect your life, then you need to find someone else who gets it and who knows how to do it.

Exercise: Chakra Balancing

The details of this exercise are found in the text above. This exercise should be used to help clear minor blockages from your energy system, but also can be used to diagnose where you have major blockages that require help from trained and experienced energy practitioners.

Invite joy into your life

Since the ultimate goal of this entire approach is to bring more happiness and joy into your experience, we need to make sure that you are prepared and able to receive them. As I have talked about making sure that your energy is able to tune in to communication from Spirit, we also must make sure that your energy is open to receiving and amplifying the energies of happiness and joy.

Many of us have become so closed off, so removed from our place of joy that even during those times when we do feel happiness, excitement or passion, we can't truly experience it or express it. This is how I have felt most of my life. In my case, I always stopped myself from feeling and expressing joy and excitement because I felt like if I actually enjoyed something it would make me vulnerable. Because then someone might use it as a weapon against me. Even when I was happy and proud of myself, or very excited about something, I would hide it or talk down about it. Because of this I would never really experience happiness. Anytime I would tell Anni that I was the happiest that I had ever been, she would respond that there was no way for her tell and she would repeatedly tell me that my emotional expressions did not reflect happiness or joy to her in any way. So, this inability to feel or express happiness not only robbed me of joy, it also affected my relationships and how I was viewed by other people.

So how can one break out of this joyless prison? The first step is always to set the intention to invite joy back into your being. Be clear about your desire and look for ways to do it. Personally, I found that two physical practices made a huge difference in opening me up from the place where all joy and excitement were immediately quashed to now where I can laugh and be excited with ease. I can even sing a little bit now. These practices are: (1) smile and (2) laugh. The simple act of making eye contact with people as I pass them, smiling and saying hello was difficult for me at first and took focused effort. But within a few days the smiles came much more easily and I was already opening up. Similarly, I tried to laugh as hard and as often as possible. This practice would help to acclimate my body to the energies of happiness and unbridled joy. To this end, every television show or movie that I watched during this period was a comedy, the funnier the better. I would have to say that the movie Wedding Crashers has been very important to my spiritual growth as I can always count on laughing to the point of tears for two straight hours every time I watch it. Even now, watching the Daily Show with John Stewart every day is as much a part of my practice as is yoga or meditation. When you are happy, you smile and laugh and smiling and laughing gets you in the habit of being happy.

The purpose of all of this work on your energy is to prepare you for the real work of changing your underlying beliefs and attitudes about the world and your role in it. It helps you to loosen up emotional blocks caused by old wounds so that you can overcome your deeply held assumptions. Raising your energy level also allows you to be better able to "tune in" to the help and guidance available to you from your intuition, higher self or spirit guides. This brings us to the next aspect of our happiness workout...

Listen for guidance

We all have unique paths to travel in our lives. We all have our own purpose for being here, our own issues to meet and overcome and our own set of lessons (read challenges) to experience. As a result, there is no one size fits all plan to guide us through our lives step by step. However, we do have access to completely individualized guidance from Spirit, or what I often refer to as our higher selves.

This source of wisdom and help derives from outside of the physical world, so we can't hear it with our ears. It can come in many forms, however, the most common forms are intuition and inspiration. Most of us won't receive guidance from a vision of a floating Jesus or a burning bush that is telling us what to do. We will feel the information. The challenge for us with this mode of communication is that we have been taught not to believe anything that is not the result of rigorous intellectual analysis or deduction. As a result, most of the time that we have a feeling about what we should do or if we are inspired with a great idea, we just ignore it. Thus, our job is to not only reconnect with our intuition and inspiration, but also to learn to trust it so that we may then act on it.

Our first job is to be able to hear the help that is being offered to us. The first step to effective listening in any situation is to stop talking. In this case, this means to break the flow of the constant monologue going on in our heads from our "thinking" minds. When our minds are clogged up with constant thoughts about what has happened in our lives, what could happen, all of the people who have wronged us, all of the tasks we have to get done, all of the things we don't like, etc., then there is no space to be able to receive guidance. This is why all spiritual and religious traditions, especially the mystical sects within each tradition, include some form of meditation or prayer.

Having practiced some form of both mediation (from a Buddhist perspective) and prayer (from a Christian perspective) I have experienced the strengths and some limitations of both. As I studied some Buddhism, my understanding of how to do meditation was to sit and let the mind become quiet. In this tradition, I was taught that it was of key importance not to go into meditation with any intentions or desires for specific experiences or outcomes, but to just "be". Using this approach I was able to have some very pleasant experiences, as my mind quieted I felt a strong connection with the divine, which brought me great peace in the moment and I would carry "echoes" of this peace back out with me into regular life. While I was sitting in meditation, I was becoming open and in tune with the divine. However, when in this state, if any thoughts, ideas or inspiration came to me, I was supposed to let them go, as the purpose of the exercise was to be in the quiet peaceful state. I am as big of a fan of the Buddha as anyone, but to travel this path towards enlightenment seemed to require that one leaves his or her worldly life and retreat to a monastery to sit in mediation many hours every day. Thus, to reach the state of happiness and joy on a daily basis, regardless of what was going on seemed to require that I spend a lifetime in meditation. This didn't seem very practical to me in this lifetime where I have a family and many other people who count on me every day. In addition, while I felt drawn towards a spiritual practice like this, it just didn't make logical sense or feel right that I would be born into a certain life and yet, the only way to enlightenment was to avoid the relationships and stresses that come along with it? I felt that I needed more.

As a child growing up in a Christian tradition, my idea of prayer was to come up with a laundry list of things to ask God for (if I asked for more things for other people than for myself all the better). So basically this practice would become something like, God please: help me to get a girlfriend, help so and so to get over their illness, help the Eagles beat the Cowboys, Redskins and Giants this year, please help me to get an A on my Physics exam even though I didn't study and, oh yeah, please help anyone with anything that I forgot to ask for. Amen. Not surprisingly, this wasn't especially effective for me. While I think the best thing about this approach is that I did go into it with specific intentions, the main problems were that most of my requests were for petty things that, even if they happened, wouldn't substantially increase my happiness in life and also, once I got done making my requests, I went back to my regular life. I never stopped to listen to see if maybe God was trying to answer my prayers directly to me. So I didn't continue with this practice for very long.

I have found a practice that does work for me that combines some aspects of both meditation and prayer as described above. I view meditation as an opportunity for me to receive communication from Spirit. However, I have found it most effective when I go into a session with a set of clear intentions. First, I invite any spirit guides in and ask for that they help me. Next, I intend that I will be open to hear the guidance that is given me, and lastly, if I have any specific problem or issue that I am seeking help with, I put that on the table as well. For example, I may be worried about being able to pay the rent next month so I will ask the spirit guides to help me to understand this situation better, what I can learn from it and how I should best proceed. Once I have planted these seeds I sit, as with a traditional Buddhist meditation, I follow my breath in and out and bring my attention to the here and now. After I feel centered I perform the exercise described above for raising energy during meditation.

I find that this exercise can raise the energy in my body and make it easier for me to receive the guidance. After this exercise is done, just sit in silence. Follow your breath in and out and envision yourself completely open as a receiver. If you find that your mind wanders back to your worries, day to day life, or what you are going to get back to doing as soon as you are finished meditating, then just take a deep breath, leave those thoughts behind and return to the silence. However, if you start to get inspired ideas, especially in relation to your original intentions, don't try to shut them off. Have a journal with you and jot them down, go with them. Remember, the entire point of this meditation is to receive help and guidance from spirit, so once you start getting it, don't stop it, just go with it. If you don't receive any specific inspiration during your meditation time, don't worry about it. But, as you go through the rest of your day try to keep a focus on being open and recognizing the ideas or inspiration when they come and always have some paper and a pencil available to jot something down that may occur to you during the day.

Each night before you go to bed, take 5-10 minutes to review your notes either from your morning meditation or anything that has come up during the day. This can help put you back in an open frame of mind before going to sleep at night. Your dreams are another great place to receive guidance from spirit. Before you go to sleep make the clear intention that you are going to remember your dreams when you wake up and jot down everything that you remember as soon as you wake up. I have gotten a lot of great ideas from my dreams.

As I have traveled down my own path to spiritual and personal growth I encountered many points along the way where even though I felt like I was making progress, I still wasn't connecting with my purpose. I felt adrift and directionless without any real anchor of where all of this was supposed to be going. Some of my own personal issues and old wounds were so deep and pervasive that they were blocking my ability to understand my destiny (even though I was able to glimpse pieces of it) and certainly I wasn't able to meet my destiny. In my particular case I knew that I loved to teach, but I wasn't interested in teaching any of the things that I was "expert" at (engineering, math, science, business, etc). Moreover, I was really gaining a deep understanding of my own spiritual nature, the meaning of life and why I was mired in anxiety, depression and suffering. However, it never occurred to me that I could be a writer and teacher of these things. My own beliefs that I was not enlightened enough or spiritual enough to become one of these people, plus my fear of taking the risk of putting myself out in this way held me back from getting into the flow of my life and destiny.

Up to this point in the Happiness Workout I have talked about preparations to make to help you to set a focus in your life, raise your energy so that you can receive spiritual guidance and begin to take steps in the direction of your life's purpose. While these are important and valuable steps, it is all still preparation, so now I will talk about how to live in your life's flow. How do you actually change your mind, alter the way that you view the world, your life and the things that happen in it to release the stress and anxiety that cause unhappiness and depression and allow you to experience the natural joy, happiness and bliss of being alive. So let's jump right in.

Practice Generosity

Be generous with your time, your money, your attention and your love. Giving to others is a very important way to begin to dismantle the idea that we are all separate and unconnected. Start with little things, offer help to someone who looks like they could use it, give someone who is lost directions, help a person who is having trouble at the gas pump, buy lunch for a homeless person. Do things with no expectation or even desire for payback or reciprocity. If the person who you are helping offers you money or anything else but their sincere gratitude, tell them that they can repay you by paying forward the gesture by helping someone else when they are in need. Once you start looking for opportunities to help people, you will find plenty of them.

As you begin to develop your generosity muscle you will find that it feels great to help other people. This is because, even though it seems like there is nothing in it for you, we are all connected and a good deed and expression of love, compassion and respect for another pays back to you ten fold. You will also find that as you become more generous with others, you will also become more generous with yourself and the more that you give, the more that you receive. However, in many places in our culture people are not used to having someone sincerely offer to help them with no expectation of reward and they may be mistrustful of your offer. If you find this to be the case, remember, the benefit to you does not accrue from the reaction or gratitude from the person who you are offering the help, but from the spirit and attitude with which you offer. So if someone refuses your help, do not try to force it on them or hold any negative feelings towards them. Remember that they are victims of their own mistrust and are missing out on help because of it. Offer them the gift of your silent love and respect and move on. A recurring theme in this section of the book is that you cannot control others so the important thing for you to do is to act with integrity, generosity and love and let the rest of the circumstances fall where they may.

Exercise: Be Generous

At least once a day surprise someone with a gift that they are not expecting. Pay for the person's coffee behind you at the Starbucks drive thru, give a flower to the receptionist at your office, help someone get something off of the top shelf at the grocery store, stop and help someone who has a flat tire. Perform the act as a complete give away with no desire or expectation of reward and if offered ask only that the recipient of your gift "pay it forward" and give help to someone else.

Practice gratitude

I have a sign in my home that says, "In all things, give thanks." The attitude of gratitude is certainly not a new concept. However, most teachings of it that I have seen are focused on raising one's consciousness of all of the "gifts" and "things to be thankful for" in one's life and to remember them often with a feeling of thankfulness in their hearts. This is a great start, but it seems to me that this approach often inherently assumes that if there is good stuff that you should be grateful for, then there is also bad stuff that you aren't grateful for. These bad things would include illness, misfortune, death, failure, etc. However, my sign says "In all things…" which means that everything that happens (what we consider good and what we consider bad) are all deserving of our gratitude. This goes back to my earlier idea that everything that happens in our life was put there by us (or our higher selves) to teach us and to help us to grow towards a permanent state of happiness and bliss. Therefore, everything, even those things that feel uncomfortable, that we would try to avoid at any cost, is here for our benefit and deserves our gratitude.

Exercise: Be Grateful

Each night before bed make a mental list of things that you cherish in life and make the conscious effort to appreciate and be grateful for each of them. Then make a quick mental list of the most difficult, challenging and unpleasant things that happened to you during the day and make the conscious effort to be grateful for them too. Take a few moments to think about how the "bad" events could really be gifts for you, but even if you can't see how they could help, just trust that they occurred for your benefit and feel and express gratitude for their help. Remember, we are in the process of retraining your mind and how you look at things so please make a strong effort to generate the feeling of gratitude and let it penetrate your entire body and being for those few minutes before bed.

Meet your fears

"There is nothing to fear, but fear, itself."
--Franklin D. Roosevelt

Fear is the single biggest roadblock to your happiness. Fear and happiness are mutually exclusive; you cannot have one where the other is present. In addition, your fears are markers pointing you to wounds that need healing or incorrect attitudes that need correction for you own growth and evolution. Fear is always a result of obscuring the truth or a misunderstanding of reality, because, in truth, there is nothing to fear. Due to this fact, the best way to deal with fear is to meet it head on and to shine the bright light of your attention and consciousness on it.

As a younger man, I was afraid of many things: what others would think of me, of making mistakes, of being exposed, of failing, just to name a few. These fears were like chains that bound me to my unhappiness, keeping me from experiencing true freedom or joy because I was always worried about something, trying to control some situation or putting up a wall around myself to prevent myself from possibly being exposed. This ensured my continued battle with depression as I watched life from the sidelines.

In 2000, I went back to school full-time to earn an MBA at Pepperdine University. When I first got there I heard a presentation on an opportunity to go on a foreign exchange program and study in a different country for a semester. When I first heard about it I remember thinking that there was no way I would ever have the guts to go to a country where I wasn't fluent in the language and try to live for four months. Insanity. But, as time wore on I met the guys who had gone on exchange to Barcelona, Spain the year before and I started thinking that if these guys could do it and survive then I certainly could. Plus a good friend and classmate of mine put out an open invitation to come visit him at his family home in India over the summer. So one day, while sitting in a presentation during a mentoring program I became especially inspired and I announced to my group that I was going to apply for the exchange program to Barcelona and that I was going to stop in India on the way. Needless to say, the next days and weeks I was having serious second thoughts, but at that point, I felt like I couldn't go back on my commitment, so I went about getting prepared to go. I bought a backpack, sold my car and put all of my belongings that I couldn't carry in a storage locker. One of the things that I was supposed to do before I left the country was to make sure that someone had all of my information, passport number, visa information, etc in case I lost any of them while traveling. So I sent all of the information to my parents with a long melodramatic letter giving them instructions on how I wanted my body cremated and that if I died, not to worry, that I was as happy as I had ever been and thought that I had a pretty good life. I was so scared of stepping out onto this new experience that I actually thought I was going to die on the trip and had to come to terms with my own mortality in order to get on the plane to go.

Of course, in hindsight, this was ridiculous. I visited my friend in New Delhi for 2 weeks and certainly had some interesting adventures but nothing life threatening. Then I was off to Barcelona for four months and had a great experience, made new lifelong friends and learned an incredible amount. I returned to the USA a different person. I had faced my fear and found out that there was nothing there to be afraid of in the first place. So not only did I learn about travel and living abroad, I also learned the true meaning of Franklin Roosevelt's famous line.

This particular experience exposed a lot of my own personal issues. My lack of self-esteem caused me to give my power away to other people's perceptions of me. I was afraid to go into an unfamiliar environment because if I did something wrong or against custom, their resulting disapproval of me would be too painful to bear. As ridiculous as this may sound to you, this is how I lived most of my life up until age 30. Thus, I needed to over-plan and try to control all aspects of my life that required venturing out into unknown territory, such as driving across the Bay Bridge in San Francisco, or taking public transit. This was so much stress and effort that I just wanted to stay home all of the time. By forcing myself to meet these fears in one trip, so many of these issues dissolved as I proved to myself that I wouldn't fall apart in unfamiliar circumstances and that I could navigate the world (literally). Imagine the change in consciousness that we all could experience if we took the 10 things that we fear the most and addressed them straight on.

Exercise: **Fear-Outs**

Make a list of the 10 things that you fear most. These are situations, people or actions that make you uncomfortable, that you avoid, that you would never consider doing. It could be as simple as avoiding eye contact and saying "Hi" when you pass someone in the hallway to being terrified to fly in an airplane. Then, make a plan to do them all. As you address each one keep a journal and write about the issues underlying the fear. Why does this make you afraid? What are you afraid will happen? Then, after you have met the fear in action, write about what you learned and how you view your fear differently.

Forgive and release your victimhood

"To err is human; to forgive is divine."
--Alexander Pope

Forgiveness is the lynch pin of the entire process of taking control of your happiness. By forgiving people's actions and other events that occur you are no longer at their mercy for how you feel; you control your own mental and emotional state.

As I start to explain how this works, we need to realize that the type of forgiveness that I am talking about is NOT where you excuse, condone or do not hold someone accountable for their actions. The type of forgiveness that I am talking about here has absolutely nothing to do with who or what you are forgiving and everything to do with you. In this way, forgiveness is actually release. You are releasing the choice to feel angry, victimized, hurt or offended. By releasing these feelings and your need to have these feelings in any circumstance, then you become invulnerable, you cannot be hurt.

A quick example to illustrate the point. When my stepson Zoë was about 6 years old he had to have some dental surgery that required he undergo a strong anesthetic. The dentist said that until Zoë slept for an hour he would be a bit cranky. For the entire 15 minute drive home Zoë was yelling at me from the back seat of the car that I was driving too slow, I was driving too fast, I was going the wrong way and then he culminated with, "Tim! You are the worst driver in the world!"

Normally, a commentary like this from anyone would have gotten me mad. However, in this case, I just let it pass right through and I held no anger or frustration around it because I knew that he was under the influence of the anesthetic and not trying to hurt or criticize me. The fact that I did not hold onto any negative feeling around this episode was an act of forgiveness, and in this act, I was able to avoid the negative emotions that erode happiness and result in anger and depression. Having immediately forgiven, I was able to continue my flow of love and compassion for this young boy as he recovered from his trip to the dentist.

This type of forgiveness is nothing new, whether you call it forgiveness, quantum forgiveness, nonattachment, nonjudgment, it is the same as was taught by Jesus, Buddha and many others before and since. However, the key for me in learning to apply it has been to figure out a new way to look at the "bad" stuff that happens to me that facilitates my ability to release the negative emotions. In the example above, what allowed me to let the insults and criticisms go was that Zoë was drugged out and in pain. Therefore, I told myself, he was not in full control of his faculties so I decided not to react and not to give his words any power over me. Now, for this purpose, it doesn't really matter if he truly does feel that I am the worst driver in the world, but the important thing is that I find the best way for me to keep the power over how I feel and not give it away to anybody or anything.

How to practice forgiveness

I have found two primary ways of looking at things to be most effective in helping me to forgive the things that really get under my skin in life and I often am able to combine the two. I have been fortunate enough (I guess that is one way to look at it!) to have plenty of forgiveness opportunities including: hating my job, getting a divorce, losing a job, being attacked with lies and falsehoods, financial struggle, collapse and ruin, repossession of cars, being told that I am wrong, being told that I am incompetent and being told that I lack integrity, called fat, called ugly just to name a few (and that was just this morning). We all have our similar lists, mine happen to revolve mainly around career and finances, but it could just as easily be about personal relationships, family, health, etc. In the end we all have our challenges, that is why we are here.

The two aspects of my thought system that help me to forgive are: (1) that everything happens for a reason that benefits me and (2) when the forgiveness opportunity involves another person to look deeply into the cause of the anger or fear that motivated them and to put myself in their shoes. These can essentially be summarized as (1) meaning and (2) compassion. So the meaning that I see in all things is the essence of the thought system that I described in the beginning of this book. I am pure spirit and the reason that I am having the experience of this life on earth is for my spirit to heal the wounds of separation and to realize my boundless creative power as the divine. Heck, anything that is helping me do something that awesome should be received in complete gratitude and not resisted in pain and anxiety. The most powerful aspect of this point of view for me is that this is something that I planned for myself as spirit. Each event is so important for me that I brought it upon myself. This is like the tennis player training to play in a tournament who sets up one of those little ball machines that shoots balls over the net for practice. The player doesn't curse the balls and ask God why they keep coming at her. She just keeps hitting them back over the net, improving and honing her skills, thankful for the opportunity to practice that will help her towards her goal of winning the tournament. The approach of finding a deeper meaning in everything can work for anything that happens in life that causes you discomfort.

The second aid for me in my forgiveness work is a desire to develop compassion for the person who seems to be screwing me over. At this point in my life, it feels like I have made just about every mistake, every error and acted out of every negative emotion possible. This gives me a very good foundation to look deeply into what is motivating other people and then relate it back to my own experience. I find that if I can relate someone's actions to something that I, myself, have done in the past, then it is easier for me to find compassion and understanding and then, easier for me to forgive and release.

For example, when my business and personal finances really went down the tubes, we were renting a house in West Los Angeles. Our arrangement had been to make our rent payments by directly depositing a check into our landlord's bank account. As our situation became more dire and we ran out of people to borrow rent money from we started to fall behind on our payments. As it turns out, our landlord wasn't doing a very effective job of tracking our payments and we fell much further behind than he realized. However, as his financial situation became more stressed and he started to look closer at our rent payments he became very angry and evicted us from the house. Our financial situation did not improve and then we weren't able to make the settlement payments to him to pay off the back rent. This bothered our landlord so much that he called my cell phone and left a very nasty message in which he insulted me, called me names and accused me of fraud and other crimes. Normally, anytime someone attacked me or accused me of such things it would penetrate me deeply, make me feel sick to my stomach and would be something that I would carry with me all the time and far into the future. However, I realized that he was acting out of anger. He obviously was feeling financial strain and he saw me as at least a partial cause of that strain and he was frustrated that he was not getting any money out of me. I am sure that he was feeling pressure from his family, his business partners, his creditors and everyone else and that he was feeling fear that he would not be able to meet his commitments. I could understand all of these things as I had been going through all of the same type of financial challenges and fears. I know how upsetting and out of control this can make you feel so, much like the case where I attributed a situation to the effects of anesthetic, I was able to attribute this situation to the effects of fear and anxiety. This allowed me to take control of my feelings and not allow that message to penetrate me or to make me feel badly. This certainly did not mean that I condoned his reaction or his approach with me, just as if our situations were reversed, when I forgave the person who did not pay me, that would not mean that I would condone or defend not following through on commitments or even necessarily release a person from their commitments, but I would release its hold on my happiness and I would be able to move forward free of negative emotion and anxiety fully ready to meet the world and live in joy. This is the essence of forgiveness and release.

Exercise: **Practice Forgiveness**

Any time and every time that something happens in life that causes you stress, pain or inconvenience, use this forgiveness practice so that: (1) you react to the circumstances and the people involved in the incident in a way that helps you grow towards wholeness and (2) you are able to process and release any anger, bitterness or other negative feelings.

When you first start to become aware of feelings of resistance, anger, fear or other negative emotion towards a person or situation, take a deep breath and remember the following things:

- The outcome of a specific situation is not the important thing ("winning" vs. "losing", "success" vs. "failure"). Everything is a means to one end only and that end is learning and growth towards wholeness and unlimited happiness and joy.

- This particular situation is a gift that you have given to yourself in order to learn a valuable lesson. Try to figure out what the lesson or opportunity is and then learn it. If you can't figure out the lesson, then trust that there is one and try to participate in the situation in a way that brings you towards love and wholeness and away from attack, fear and separation.

- That this situation is just one of many that you have experienced over thousands of lifetimes, and even though you play a particular role in this one, at one time or another you have played every role, you have been the rich one and the poor one, the healthy one and the sick one, the calm one and the hysterical one, the oppressor and the oppressed. Since you could easily fall into a situation where you could play one of the other roles, then it is easier not to judge the other harshly, to feel some compassion for their situation and state of mind and not stay focused on how they should be different. Just bring your focus back to the fact that there are a variety of personal and environmental factors that cause any situation and while you certainly do not need to accept all of them as appropriate, it brings you great peace and strength to be able to accept that it is what it is and move forward from there.

By giving meaning to the events, accepting them as they are, trusting that everything is working out exactly as it should for you, and having compassion for all involved, including yourself, you can greatly shorten the duration of and eventually completely eliminate the negative feelings and emotions that we now experience when life doesn't go as we think it should.

Since this is such a critical exercise, I offer here a couple of experiences from my own life and how these forgiveness principles can be (and in some cases were) applied here for the most benefit.

After I was fired from my consulting job and prior to the baby food company starting up I had a part time gig where I taught test preparation courses to people who were applying for graduate school. I was a pretty effective teacher, I enjoyed helping the students and I got good reviews, so everything was going along fine. Then, one day in the middle of a new session of courses all of the sudden it felt like I hit a wall. The courses were generally held in classrooms at UCLA in the evenings, which was about a 15-20 minute drive from my home. I started hitting a streak of freak traffic situations where I would get within a mile or so of the UCLA campus and would be stopped dead in gridlock traffic. It began taking me 1 – 2 hours to get to class. One time I attributed it to a basketball game on campus. Another night just as I was leaving and going to drop one of Zoë's friends off at home on the way and the kids covered themselves in paints just as we were supposed to leave. So by the time I got them cleaned up and dropped off his friend, fought traffic, again, I was very late for class. This happened about 3 or 4 class sessions in a row, there didn't seem to be any way that I could get to class on time no matter how hard I tried. So, not surprisingly, one of the students started to complain and wanted a refund for the course. As a reaction to this, when I showed up to teach the class one evening, the owner of the company was waiting for me outside of the classroom with a check and informed me that I was being put on disciplinary suspension.

My first reaction was anger. I was angry at the owner of the company for the way he handled the situation, I was angry at the student who complained, I was angry at the forces that had kept me from getting to class on time, I was angry at myself for not leaving 3 hours early, and on and on. Plus, even though it was a part time job that did not pay much, I was scared of losing that contribution to our income. However, once I got home and talked about it with Anni I was able to start processing the situation in a more productive manner.

I knew that something was happening when I kept running into these roadblocks that prevented me from getting to class on time. It was abundantly clear that some greater force was at work because it didn't seem plausible that I could run into these problems so many times in a row as a coincidence. Therefore, it was easier for me to see this situation as coming to me for a reason, even if I didn't know what it was. I was then able to apply a positive meaning to it and be able to accept it for what it was and not continue to play mind games in how the situation should have turned out differently. I wasn't able to see the lessons for me in that moment, but over time I have come to understand that so many of these trials for me during that period were about trust and developing my ability to trust that things were working out as they should, even if I couldn't see the master plan. Plus, losing that job also opened up more room in my life to be able to launch the baby food company.

Another area where I didn't perform well in that situation was that I had very little success in having compassion for the owner of the company as he threw me out of my job with no warning. I struggled for quite a while with negative feelings towards him. This related to my issues with self-esteem, which resulted in me being hyper-sensitive to criticism – none of which I was able to see at the time.

This example shows that, at the time, I did have some awareness that I was having this particular experience for a reason and showed that I made attempts to try and figure it out and learn the lessons. However, it also shows that while I was trying to be open to all of the lessons available, I still had some significant issues to work out and I wasn't able demonstrate complete learning of all of the lessons available. But, I was able to learn the lessons eventually, which also shows that sometimes the lessons from an incident aren't fully learned or appreciated until sometime in the future from the actual events. This is also an excellent example of why this book is called Practicing Happy and not Perfectly Happy. We are all on a path of growth and none of us are going to be perfect. We just need to make sure that we continue to work at it, develop our strengths and skills and we will reap the benefits as we grow. Just as a review, here is my view of the ideal way that I could have reacted in this situation:

• I would have recognized that this is a situation given to me as a learning opportunity and the fact that I was being removed from my job was not the most important aspect, but that I needed to learn the appropriate lessons.

• I would have accepted that this situation had happened as it should have and not spent a lot of time and energy on what ifs and what I and everyone else could and should have done differently.

• I would have trusted that I was supposed to leave this job at this time and that there was a larger reason for it. I also would have trusted that other opportunities would follow to fill in for this job so I would need to be looking for them and ready to take advantage of them when they appeared.

• I would have had more compassion for myself and the owner of the company. I would have accepted that I tried very hard to get to class on time and the fact that I wasn't able to for those few weeks did not make me a bad person or to blame for the overall circumstances. Similarly, I would have looked more deeply and seen that the owner of the company was reacting to the situation as he saw it and while I could still feel that he could have handled the situation in a more positive, sensitive and productive manner, I could have realized that he has his own issues that he is working through and not judge him for where he was anymore than I should have been judging myself for where I was at the time.

Again, these are ideals that are much easier to talk about in hindsight than in the moment, but gives you an idea of where we are hoping to go with this training program.

Now, just for fun, I thought that I would share with you pretty much the most difficult day of my life. After the collapse of our baby food company it took me over a year to find full time employment again as a contract project manager for a marketing and training company. In the first few months I was thrown in as a key player on a project to develop some new training courses for a major client. It was on a very challenging timeline, but we met the objectives and had our two day demonstration of the classes for the client scheduled. The first day came off well and I was at the end of about two weeks of working 18-20 hour days, so with just one more day to go, I felt good and decided to go home for a few hours sleep. However, I was nervous about leaving our presentation equipment at the hotel, so I packed everything up in my car and took it home with me. Since it was after 1 AM by the time I got home and I was leaving again at 5 AM for the hotel, I just left everything in the car parked in front of my house.

You may be able to guess this, but when I walked out in front of my house at 5 AM to leave, my car was gone along with about $25,000 worth of the company's presentation equipment and the entire set up for the client presentation. My heart sunk to my feet. I literally considered just walking away from the presentation from the company and from my job and just giving up. After a few deep breaths I got on the phone with my supervisor back in Detroit and started waking people up and letting them know that my car was stolen with everything inside. Needless to say once the disbelief passed and everyone figured out that I wasn't playing a practical joke on them, I wasn't the most popular guy on the team. As I waited for one of my colleagues to drive up from Orange County (about an hour away) to pick me up and take me down to help try to figure out the day, I decided to walk the two blocks to the local police station to report my car stolen. The desk officer looked up the license plate on his computer and informed me that the car was not stolen, but was repossessed because I was behind on my payments. This was even worse news. At least when my car was stolen there was some air that I was a victim and not completely at fault, but with the car being repossessed all of the responsibility fell squarely on my shoulders. But, the one bright spot was that at least I had a chance to try to recover the equipment in the back as long as the repo man was honest or didn't realize that I had all those electronics in the back.

So I slogged back to my house and called back my boss to let him know the situation. At this point, everything broke down. All of the stress of the previous few years, of not having a steady or sufficient income, of the rise and destruction of my business, the stress of raising children without health insurance, it all came to a focal point and I completely broke down crying on the phone with him. He was remarkably compassionate and supportive of me (which was not his reputation at work), but after hanging up I finally took a few minutes to reflect on my situation, remove myself from the stress and emotion of the moment and begin to look for some meaning.

I had been working with this material long enough to know what I needed to do, the challenge was being able to do it. Clearly, the fact that the car was repossessed with no warning on the one day that I had all of that material in it for a client presentation was part of some larger plan. I knew that it was a lesson, and suspected strongly that it was an opportunity to see how well I could practice forgiveness on something that felt like a pretty big deal. The situation also challenged me to see if I had the discipline to speak and act with honesty and integrity even though the truth was incredibly embarrassing and made me look pretty bad and would probably lead me to getting fired that day (i.e. would I get caught up in the outcome rather than focusing on the learning). I also took compassion on myself and didn't beat myself up over what I could/should have done differently. I simply accepted that this needed to happen in this way because it was a lesson/test that I needed to experience. So at this point I was able to let go of attachment to the outcome, I sent an email to my team letting them know that the car was repossessed and that I might be able to get some of the equipment back by lunch time.

Then, an amazing thing happened. Everyone else on the team was able to pull together and they completely recreated the complex technical set up and pulled off the client presentation to rave reviews. I wasn't able to contribute much that day, but they were all very supportive of me and I didn't get fired. Looking back I truly believe that I was able to handle this situation well enough that the universe gave me a passing grade, which then allowed the day to flow. Everyone was happy, I got all of the company's equipment back and my company even lent me a car for a few days until I could raise the money to get my car out of hock.

This incident taught me that these practices can work in even the most intense and difficult of circumstances. I can't say that I was in my happy place throughout that day, but I can say that I was able to cope with a potentially highly stressful situation in a way that did not cause me a high level of anxiety and I was able to recover from my down moments very quickly. After weathering this experience, I feel incredibly strong and capable maintaining my peace and joy in almost any situation.

CHAPTER 7

WRAPPING IT ALL UP

The primary focus of our work here in human form is to expand our view of everyday life to include the fact that we are spiritual beings and that events and our lives are influenced not only by our intentions and actions here in the physical world, but also the plans and intentions that our souls put into place prior to our birth. We each came into this life with specific plans for the types of experiences that we wanted to have, the skills and abilities that we wanted to develop for ourselves, and the work that we wanted to do to help others. These plans and intentions set the stage for our lives and influence the types of circumstances and events that we experience. The key to happiness and fulfillment in life is simple, when we act in accordance with these pre-birth plans, then we are in the flow of our lives, but when we act in ways that take us away from our destiny, we are out of the flow and we will feel lonely, anxious and depressed. So the keys to happiness are simple (1) remember that you are pure spirit and you chose to have this life experience in order to grow and learn, (2) remember that every experience that you have in this life was planned by you for your own ultimate benefit (3) there is specific work that you intended to do in this life to help yourself and to help others, you must find it and do it. Once you begin to understand and integrate this new point of view you will be released from all fear. You stop resisting challenging events and begin to look for the beauty and gift in them. You stop worrying about your future as you gain confidence that there is a reason and plan for all things. You are able to free yourself from your thoughts that keep you from pursuing and performing work that you love and that is meaningful to you.

The challenge is that these three keys, for many of us, are not how we live our lives now, nor are they what we were taught since birth. As a result, changing our fundamental beliefs about the meaning and substance of our lives is necessary to achieve happiness. This is where the practicing comes in. I have described a spiritual happiness workout that can help you to break your habits, change your mind and open you to the joy and inner peace that you were born to have.

the author

 TIM DAULTER, a native of Philadelphia, PA earned a BS in Chemical Engineering and Engineering and Public Policy from Carnegie Mellon University and a PhD in Chemical Engineering from the University of Delaware. Six years of working as an engineer for the DuPont Company finally convinced him that he was on the wrong path. As a result of many personal struggles he ventured to California where he earned an MBA from Pepperdine University. After meeting his wife Anni and the birth of their first child together, they were inspired to create an Organic Baby Food Company. This experience proved both rewarding and challenging, and although he valued the lessons he received, he knew that his calling was for a more spiritual life. He began to discover the spiritual teachings that further deepened his spark of self awareness and led him down a path of self improvement and spiritual growth that has given him the greatest gift of all - the ability to be happy. Although he has often been a reluctant student in learning and living the principles laid out in this book, the stunning transformation that he experienced over a period of a few years inspired him to share the gifts that were given to him with as many people as possible.

Tim currently resides in Chester Springs, PA with his amazing family of Anni, Zoë, Lotus Sunshine, Bodhi Ocean and River Love.

Made in the USA
San Bernardino, CA
25 January 2015